Christ-Following

Christ-Following

Ten Signposts to Spirituality

TREVOR HUDSON

FOREWORD BY GORDON MACDONALD

Fleming H. Revell

A Division of Baker Book House Co
Grand Rapids, Michigan 49516

© 1996 by Trevor Hudson

Published by Fleming H. Revell
a division of Baker Book House Company
P.O. Box 6287, Grand Rapids, MI 49516-6287

Printed in the United States of America

Library of Congress Cataloging-in-Publication Data

Hudson, Trevor, 1951–
     Christ-following : ten signposts to spirituality /
Trevor Hudson.
          p.   cm.
     Includes bibliographical references.
     ISBN: 0-8007-5575-8 (pbk.)
     1. Christian life. 2. Spirituality. I. Title.
BV4501.2.H766 1996
248.4—dc20   95-46612

Unless otherwise indicated, Scripture quotations are taken from the New Revised Standard Version of the Bible (NRSV), copyright 1989 by the Division of Christian Education of the National Council of Churches of Christ in the USA. Used by permission.

Scripture marked NIV is taken from the HOLY BIBLE, NEW INTERNATIONAL VERSION®. NIV®. Copyright © 1973, 1978, 1984 by International Bible Society. Used by permission of Zondervan Publishing House. All rights reserved.

Other versions cited are Today's English Version (TEV), New English Bible (NEB), and the King James Version (KJV).

To Debbie
Faithful friend and
dearest companion
along the Way

Contents

Foreword   9
Acknowledgments   13
Introduction   17

Drawing a Picture of God   21
Developing a Christian Memory   40
Receiving the Kingdom   60
Acknowledging Our Shadow Selves   77
Belonging to the Family of God   94
Becoming Holy, Becoming Ourselves   113
Loving Those Closest to Us   133
Discovering God's Call for Our Lives   149
Finding God in All Things   167
Growing into Christlikeness   186

Notes   205

Foreword

In 1991 my wife, Gail, and I were invited to South Africa to speak to conferences of Baptists, Methodists, and Anglicans. Upon arrival at the airport in Johannesburg we were met by two Christian pastors, one a Baptist, the other a Methodist. The Methodist was Trevor Hudson, the author of this wonderful book, *Christ-Following*.

I soon learned that Trevor Hudson and I would be co-speakers at one of the pastors' conferences on our schedule. That fact alone forced us together as we sounded out one another about subject matter and ministry intentions so that we would not "wander into each other's territory" (an Americanism).

I quickly learned that I was teaming up with a man younger in years but older in spiritual maturity and frankly, my observation caused me to wonder why my kind South African hosts would fly a man from the other end of the world when they had wellsprings like Trevor Hudson from which to draw.

Hudson's quiet, intense spirit was something to experience. His keen mind had absorbed a panoply of reading sources: from the desert Fathers to the spiritual masters of the Middle Ages, from the pages of the mystics to the modern thinkers and wrestlers with truth. And he had traveled, making it his purpose to sit down and listen to men and women of enormous spiritual breadth and depth.

Not only this, but Hudson had spent more than a few days with people who were in perpetual pain: the poor, the suffering, those put down by oppressive societies. He had refused the insulated, protected life, and on the hands and feet of his soul were the dirt, the scars, and the calluses of a life experience that knew suffering firsthand. If you are wise, you listen carefully to the stories and insights of a man with experiences like that.

But most of all I quickly discerned that Trevor Hudson had worked hard at knowing God, not just through the experience of others but through his own pursuit of spiritual discipline and conditioning. And it told! The days we spent together were soul-filling for me. I loved hearing him unravel Bible stories with new perspectives and possibilities that I'd not seen before. Needless to say, the man marked my life.

Now as I read the pages of this book and then go back to my journal for reminiscences of those days in South Africa, I am aware that much of the subject material was being birthed in the talks and sermons he was giving then. Like many others in the Christ-following community in 1991 Trevor Hudson was struggling with what a "new South Africa" (as they liked to say) was going to look like. Mandela had "come out" a year before (referring to that incredible day when South Africa's first black president had walked from prison a free man). Everyone was aware that massive changes were in the wind. There would soon be national elections; political extremist groups were threatening sabotage and violence; the business community was frightened for the future; rumors were often ugly. An excess of anxiety was in the air.

This then was the context for Trevor Hudson's thoughts and meditations. And they mark this book. At that time—and now on these pages—he was calling people to courage, to vision, to acts of Christian servanthood. But—and here is the thrust of this book—he was reminding all who listened that such qualities and performances are impossible without an underlying soul-strength that can be found only in constant communion with the living God.

In the four years since we were in South Africa, that country has carried out a remarkable social revolution. It has many "miles to go before . . ." but it has already gone a long, long way. And the Christian community has played a powerful role in the nation's progress toward justice and reconciliation.

There once was a time when much of the world looked with harsh eyes toward South Africa. It was easy to deplore the horrific nature of apartheid while neglecting the "logs" in our own eyes. But— and God be praised—during those dark days when the news from South Africa often seemed so bleak, God was doing a quiet work in the lives of men and women throughout the country. Men and women (from all the races) like Trevor Hudson were the kind that God was raising up. They made the difference. And now they speak to us from great depths of spirit. It would do us well to listen to what the Spirit has to say from their hearts.

Gordon MacDonald
Grace Chapel
Lexington, Massachusetts

Acknowledgments

numerous people have contributed to the writing and publishing of this book. I would like to extend to them my deep gratitude and appreciation. Without their insight, encouragement, and practical help I doubt whether this manuscript would ever have been completed.

Several years ago I had the privilege of sharing the platform with Gordon MacDonald at a National Conference for Baptist Ministers in South Africa. It was Gordon who connected me with Bill Petersen of Baker Book House, passed on to him the outline for the book, and kindly accepted the publisher's invitation to write the foreword. I am greatly in debt to him, and to Bill, for their support and guidance. I am also indebted to Gordon MacDonald for the use of the term "Christ-follower," a word he coined to describe a disciple of Christ. Special appreciation goes to Mary Suggs who brought her editing skills to bear on the manuscript in its final stages.

During the writing of this book over the past three years, two other authors have encouraged, challenged, and guided me. Morton Kelsey helped me to keep believing that I had something worthwhile to say. Taking time to read carefully each chapter and offer me his wise counsel has meant a great deal. Through his friendship and writings, Dallas Willard has considerably shaped my understanding of what it means to learn from Jesus how to live. I owe these two men an immense amount of gratitude and appreciation.

If it had not been for the friendship of Phillip Bauser during my high school years, I may never have embarked on the pilgrimage of faith. Along the Way I have been given the gifts of many good friendships with fellow pilgrims. These friends will know who they are and I thank them for all that they mean. For those who prayed for me while this book was being written I am especially grateful.

For a number of years Dr. Cliff Allwood has walked alongside me, both offering a listening presence in moments of inward struggle and supervising my own pastoral ministry. During those times when I have gone through valleys of darkness, he has held out the Christ-light for me.

Over the past fourteen years I have pastored two very special congregations—the Kempton Park and Northfield Methodist churches. Much of what I have written in this book has been learned from sharing in the lives of those who belong to these two communities. I am also deeply grateful to friends at the Church of the Saviour in Washington, D.C., for their shaping influence on my life.

What I would have done without the expertise of Lyn Meyer, I do not know. With endless patience she put onto computer my handwritten notes.

My two children, Joni and Mark, have been great friends, sacrificing some of our playtime so that I could write. And my deepest thanks go to Debbie, my wife, who has stuck with me throughout. It will be good to go to the movies together again on my day off!

Introduction

One day, during my sixteenth year, I became a Christ-follower. Those gracious words of invitation, "Follow me," rooted in a great love that had sought me from my very beginnings, burned their way into my heart and evoked both desire and response. Ever since that moment of new beginnings I have been seeking to learn from Jesus how to live the one life that I have been given. This search has connected me with the lives of many other seeking pilgrims along the way. In recent years I have come to recognize this common seeking as a widespread yearning in the hearts of men and women for a vital and real spirituality.

Spirituality is a slippery word. Some are suspicious in its presence. For those whose daily lives revolve around frantic timetables—preparing breakfast, getting children to school on time, holding down a stressful eight-to-five job, paying monthly bills, cleaning the house—the word sounds somewhat strange and impractical. It suggests another world of inactivity, passivity, and uninterrupted silences. For those whose life experiences have been scarred by the wounds of suffering and oppression, the term often suggests escapism, indifference, and uninvolvement. Indeed the word needs definition. Therefore let me clarify the specifically Christian sense in which I shall be using the word: *Spirituality refers to those convictions, attitudes, and actions in and through which the Christ-following life is shaped and given personal expression within our world today.*

Amid this widespread yearning for a vital and real spirituality there is need for careful discernment. Many expressions of spirituality doing the rounds within contemporary Christian congregations can only be described as foreign to the biblical tradition and unrelated to the spirit of the crucified and risen Lord. Often they are obsessively concerned with personal needs and reflect minimal concern for those who suffer. Alternatively, a spirituality of social struggle and involvement, which avoids the biblical imperative for personal conversion and transformation, is frequently endorsed. Such endorsement falls victim to the dangerous illusion, alive and well in our midst, that we can build a more equitable, compassionate, and just society while we remain the same and continue life as usual.

In this book I offer ten signposts for the development of a renewed spirituality that is centered in the life of Jesus (our ever-present Savior and Lord), faithful to the treasures of the diverse streams within the Christian tradition, accessible to the people living next door, interwoven with those practical concerns that constitute daily living, and also deeply related to those human struggles for justice and reconciliation taking place in the streets. I write neither as an academic theologian nor as an expert in the area of spirituality. The words that follow find their birth amid the daily tasks of washing dishes and playing with the children, the vocational commitments of breaking bread and building people, and the continual crises of a turbulent nation struggling to reconstruct itself. Within these tasks, commitments, and crises I have struggled, often unsuccessfully, to live the Christ-following life. This book is shaped by these struggles.

By now it should be clear for whom I am writing: ordinary people who seek to follow Christ within the pressures, problems, and pain of everyday life. Some may be hesitantly taking the first steps into the pilgrimage of faith; some may be well-seasoned travelers requiring fresh resourcing for the journey;

some may be discouraged and weary pilgrims almost ready to pull off the road; some may be disillusioned by the crass superficiality that passes for much Christian practice today and want to explore an alternative route. Wherever you may find yourself along the Way, may you discover in these pages some nourishing food for the journey. It is my hope that these few signposts will encourage and guide you to become more radically open to the transformation that God is able to bring about in your personal and social life. A real and vital spirituality stretches toward the transforming of your personal life and of the society in which you live, work, and play. I shall be immeasurably grateful if, in the lives of some fellow pilgrims and seekers, these signposts contribute to this transformation.

At the end of each chapter is a set of questions for a group to explore together. These questions assume that you have begun to engage with some of the issues and holy experiments discussed in the chapter you have just read. An instructive ancient proverb says: "Hear and forget, see and remember, do and understand." I hope that you will be able to read the pages that follow, along with others, and together discover a more vital and real spirituality.

Drawing a Picture of God

*T*he question surprised me. I was sitting in the plainly furnished study of a close friend and mentor. Early in his career he had served as a medical missionary ministering among the rural poor of our land. Now working as a psychiatrist and lecturer on the staff of a major medical school, he had become for me a wise companion on the spiritual journey. Over the years his listening presence at critical moments in my own pilgrimage had been a gracious gift.

"What is your picture of God?" he quietly asked. In the previous thirty minutes I had sought to describe those patterns of behavior that were leaving me bedraggled in spirit, weary in body, and withdrawn in relationship. By his careful listening my mentoring friend had created for me a safe place where I could freely share my heart. When I had finished speaking he remained silent for a while, almost as if he was listening to his own heart. Then came the surprising question.

At first the question seemed unrelated and irrelevant to the concerns I had expressed. What did my view of God have to do with crowded days, an over-scheduled appointment book, and strenuous efforts to achieve and accomplish? Surely, I thought, all that is needed is some practical counsel regarding time management and realistic goal setting. However, the question communicated my companion's clear conviction that the way we live is profoundly shaped by our picture of God. Perhaps this was also why William Temple, that great Anglican minister and spiritual leader, had once rather provocatively observed that if people live with a wrong view of God, the more religious they become, the worse the consequences will get, and eventually it would be better for them to be atheists.

In his autobiography William Barclay, known throughout the world for his helpful commentaries on Scripture, recounts a personal experience that powerfully affirms our ongoing need to examine our pictures of God. The BBC had asked Dr. Barclay to do a series of talks for radio broadcast on the subject of the miracles in the Gospels. Without denying the historicity of the Gospel records, Dr. Barclay stressed the symbolic recurrence of these miracles in contemporary life. As Jesus stilled the storm on the Sea of Galilee in A.D. 28, he continues to still the storms that rage in human hearts. When the series ended, Dr. Barclay was interviewed by the producer of the program and asked how he had come to such a view.

"I told him the truth. I told him that some years ago our twenty-one-year-old daughter and the lad to whom she would some day have been married were both drowned in a yachting accident. I said that God did not stop that accident at sea, but he did still the storm in my own heart, so that somehow my wife and I came through that terrible time still on our own two feet."

When the interview was broadcast, letters poured in. Among them was an anonymous letter from Northern Ireland. "Dear Dr Barclay. I know why God killed your daughter. It was to save her from being corrupted by your heresies." Not having the writer's address, Dr. Barclay could not respond, however much he had wanted. He writes: "If I had had that writer's address I would have written back, not in anger—the inevitable blaze of anger was over in a flash—but in pity and I would have said to him, as John Wesley said to someone, 'Your God is my devil.' The day my daughter was lost at sea there was sorrow in the heart of God."[1]

In each of our hearts and minds there is drawn our picture of God. Formed over the years through interactions with parent figures, church representatives, and our surrounding culture, it significantly influences the way we live our daily lives.

This is what I began to learn that afternoon as I sat in the study of my mentor and friend. Listening perceptively to the description of my drained condition, he had offered a spiritual diagnosis. My picture of God needed to be critically examined. There was a connection between my daily-planner-driven lifestyle and my view of God.

For the first time in my life I stopped to think about my image of God. My mentor's diagnosis proved insightful. As we shared further, the picture of God operating in my depths became clearer. Yes I did feel that I needed to earn God's grace. Yes I did believe I had to achieve his affirmation. Yes I did sense that God would withdraw his blessing if I did not measure up. Gradually it dawned on me that I had come to view God as a somewhat passive spectator, sitting in the balcony of my life, whose applause would only come in response to satisfactory performance. A dysfunctional picture of God, I was discovering, had expressed itself in a dysfunctional way of living.

When distortions creep into our pictures of God, their negative effects reverberate throughout our lives. Consider some commonly held views of God together with their usual consequences. Those who view God as an impersonal force tend toward a cold and vague relationship with him. Those who see God as a heavenly tyrant, intent on hammering anyone who wanders outside his laws, seldom abandon themselves with joy to the purposes of his kingdom. Those who imagine God to be a scrupulous bookkeeper, determined to maintain up-to-date accounts of every personal sin and shortcoming, rarely acknowledge their inner contradictions and struggles in his presence. Those who regard God as a divine candy machine (just say a prayer and you can get what you want) inevitably end up in disillusionment. Since, as author-philosopher Dallas Willard has pointed out, we live at the mercy of our ideas, we would be wise to reflect carefully on those that we have about God.

I invite you to begin immediately. For a few brief moments lay this book aside and ponder your current image of God. Try to be as honest as you can. Do you believe that God wants to relate with you personally and individually? Do you feel that God is for or against you? When life goes wrong do you assume that God is punishing you? As you reflect on these questions note any negative components in your God-picture. Can you remember from where these came? How do these negative components affect your relationship with God and your life in his service?

Our pictures of God can be redrawn. It happened for Cardinal Basil Hume, Archbishop of Westminster and well-known spiritual guide, and is illustrated in an amusing story he tells about himself. On a speaking tour of the United States, he shared how he had been raised by a good but severe mother. Constantly she would say to him: "If I see you, my son, stealing an apple from my pantry, I'll punish you." Then she would add quickly, "If you take an apple and I don't see you, Almighty God will see you, and he will punish you." It doesn't take much imagination to catch a glimpse of the harsh picture of God these words sketched in young Basil's mind! As his Christian experience matured, however, his picture of God gradually changed. Eventually he came to realize, the Cardinal testified, that God might have said to him, "My son, why don't you take two?"

A Boundless Mystery

This redrawing process begins in the scriptural affirmation that God is a boundless mystery. This does not mean that he is a giant puzzle to be fathomed out. It means simply that there is no one else like him. When the word *holy* (meaning to be separate, to be different) is used to describe God, it indicates this sense of wholly otherness. Indeed if ever we think that we finally have God all figured out, then we can be sure that we are wrong. As a professor-friend kept reminding me in my know-it-all student days: "Trevor, when you are in the presence of the real God you either shut up or fall on your face."

We are often uncomfortable and uneasy in the presence of mystery. We struggle to be involved with an ungraspable God. We feel safer when faith is confined within dogmatic formulations and tidy theories. Then we can tame God, bring him under control, and manage his workings in our world. But these attempts to control and manage cost us dearly. Our sense of wonder is exiled, our faith begins suffocating from thick layers of dull familiarity and easy answers, and our lives are emptied of surprise.

In any true picture of God there will always be room for mystery. Acknowledging God in this way gets us to take off our shoes in his presence. We begin living on tiptoe. Our lives are touched with a renewed sense of awe. And, as James Houston has observed, awe is the starting point in our quest for God. He writes: "Awe encourages us to think of God as a transcendent presence: someone outside and beyond our own small concerns and our own vulnerable lives. Awe opens us up to the possibility of living always on the brink of mystery. Awe helps us to be truly alive, fully open to new possibilities we had not envisaged before."[2]

God Is Christlike

Yet we must and can say more. The bottom line of the Christian faith is the scandalous claim that

God has stepped into human history in the person of Jesus. In Jesus, God comes close and shows us his face. The boundless Mystery is not something vague and wooly, but someone personal. Listen to Paul's confident exclamation about Jesus in the midst of his carefully worded theological letter to the Colossians: "He is the image of the invisible God. . . . For in him the fullness of God was pleased to dwell" (Col. 1:15, 19).

If we want to get our picture of God clearer, we must look in the direction of Jesus. Through word and deed, dying and rising, Jesus introduces us to what God is really like. In a famous remark Archbishop Michael Ramsay teases out the staggering implications of this claim: "God is Christlike and in him is no un-Christlikeness at all." Dare we take this seriously? Every idea and assumption that we have about God must be measured against the person of Jesus. If they are contradicted by what we have come to know about God through Jesus they need to be relinquished. If they are not contradicted, then they can safely be included in our God-picture.

This is what letter-writer John does when he puts forward his picture of God for our consideration. In the opening sentences of his first letter he reminds his readers that he writes from the perspective of one who has known firsthand the company of Jesus. On this basis he concludes a few chapters later that "God is love" (1 John 4:16). Notice carefully that he does not say that God *has* love, but rather that God *is* love. This is the very essence of who the Holy One is—extravagantly, sacrificially, passionately loving. And since this is his essential nature, this is what God is always doing—loving you and me.

Popular Catholic writer John Powell illustrates from nature the meaning of this truth for our lives.[3] He suggests that we compare God's love to the sun. It is the nature of the sun always to give off warmth and light. The sun always shines, always radiates its warmth and light. There is no way in which the sun can act against its essential nature. Nor is there any way in which we can stop it from shining. We can allow its light to fill our senses and make us warm; alternatively we can separate ourselves from its rays by putting up an umbrella or going indoors. But whatever we may do we know that the sun itself does not change.

In the same way, the God whom we see in Jesus always loves. Like the shining sun, his love never stops loving. We have the freedom to open ourselves to this love and be transformed by it or we can separate ourselves from it. But we cannot stop him from continuously sending out the warm rays of his love. At the heart of the boundless Mystery there is a blazing love that has created us, searches for us every moment, and desires to bring us, along with all of creation, into wholeness.

Jesus in Word and Deed

The words of Jesus direct us constantly toward this faithful Divine Lover. The parable of the waiting father and runaway son does this most powerfully for me. The arrogant son demands his inheritance and heads for a distant country. The father waits patiently and longingly for his return. You can imagine him each day walking to the edge of his property, watching down the road, hoping for his son's return. One day he sees the haggard figure of his son on the distant horizon and runs down the road to embrace him. Before the boy can even complete his repentance speech, his father hugs him and orders the best robe to be given to him. Here is the God who is recklessly in love with you and me, forgiving us freely before we have properly repented, and clothing us with gracious acceptance even before we have had our baths.

The deeds of Jesus wrap flesh around his words. Throughout his life he consistently reached out in friendship to those around him. In his company people from all walks of life felt accepted and welcomed. Whether it was a well-to-do public official like Zacchaeus, lepers living in forced isolation, or children simply wanting a lap to sit on, everyone seemed at home in his presence. These people-contacts often took place around mealtimes, which in the Middle East was a particularly intimate form of association. South African theologian Albert Nolan, reflecting on the impact these mealtimes would have had on those who sat at table with Jesus, writes: "Moreover because Jesus was looked upon as a man of God and a prophet, they would have interpreted his gesture of friendship as God's approval of them. They were now acceptable to God."[4]

While in these friendships and meal-sharing moments Jesus lives out the Holy One's all-inclusive love that enfolds each one of us, there is in his heart a distinctive sensitivity toward the most broken and vulnerable. Scan the Gospels and it becomes clear that Jesus invests a large percentage of his time in those who are suffering. Frequently he is to be found in the company of the sick, the mentally tormented, the poor, and the marginalized. His example reminds me of the caring mother who, when asked by a friend which of her three children she loved most, replied that she loved them all equally. Her friend refused to accept this answer and pressured her again with the same question. For a few seconds the mother became quiet and then firmly responded. "Okay, I love them all the same, but when one of them struggles and is in trouble, then my heart goes out to that child the most."

Now we can understand why God's compassionate love is sometimes accompanied by his anger. When people are deliberately hurt, God gets angry. One particular Gospel episode, the story of Jesus cleansing the temple, illustrates this angry response. Entering the temple Jesus sees that people are being exploited and excluded. He is inflamed. Making a whip of cords he scatters the wide-eyed animals, overturns the money-lenders' tables, and drives the traders out of the temple. Through these actions Jesus demonstrates how God feels about oppressive practices and unjust structures. He reveals the God of the psalmist who "executes justice for the oppressed . . . sets the prisoners free . . . lifts up those who are bowed down" (Ps. 146:7–9).

Jesus Crucified

The dying Jesus takes us deeply into the sacred mystery of God's passionate heart. Take some time to fix your eyes on this broken man nailed to the tree. Remember that he is the image of the invisible God, the one in whom God was pleased to dwell. The tortured, ravaged figure strips empty clichés and familiar sentimentality from our talk about God's love. As we stand at the foot of the cross we catch a glimpse of how God in Christ absorbs the very worst we can do, bears it sacrificially in his own body, and then responds with life-giving forgiveness. The welcome home scene of the wayward son is not too good to be true. It is as real as broken flesh and a pierced side.

Visitors to the Notre Dame chapel in Paris tell me that the front altar is flanked by two impressive statues. One is the statue of the waiting father embracing his returning son. This is the story that Jesus told. The other statue is mother Mary holding the figure of her crucified son. This is the story that Jesus lived. The story that he lived convinces us that the story he told is true. We are the beloved sons and daughters of the Father. All is forgiven. We can come home.

Contemplate once more the crucified Christ-figure hanging on the cross. Trying to comprehend the meaning of what we see stretches our capacities for understanding to their limits. God, we gradually realize, not only understands our pain but shares it. The suffering God, nailed to the tree, participates in our suffering. Alan Jones writes, "During the week of the crucifixion we have to think the unthinkable, God weeps! God suffers! God is Victim!"[5] We are never alone in our pain. It is this truth that keeps the light of faith flickering in the darkened hearts of the grieving, that renews hope in the oppressed, that empowers loving in hearts that have been betrayed and broken.

I have just learned this again from the spontaneous testimony of a courageous and grieving mother. As I write these paragraphs I'm leading a forty-eight-hour silent retreat for first-time retreatants. Moments ago I spent time listening to the prayer experience of this mother whose nineteen-year-old son died in a car accident. Her suffering is immeasurable and goes far beyond the comfort of the human word. She has been kneeling in a darkened chapel before a stark crucifix. She tells me simply: "I can face tomorrow. I know God knows and suffers with me."

Jesus Risen and Alive

But the story of Jesus' life is not over yet. On the third day his disciples and women friends find the tomb empty. Through the resurrection appearances Jesus demonstrates the death-defeating power of God's love. The lives of the disciples are turned completely around. They realize that the love that Jesus proclaimed, the love that he lived, the love that he was, can never be defeated by the powers of evil and darkness. This is the key to understanding the message of the resurrection. Easter Sunday morning is a joyful celebration of the power of God's love and its unquenchable capacity to bring life out of death.

Much testimony today is given to the power of God. Constantly those who testify create the impression that whenever God's power is at work, life is successful and prosperous. Reflecting on these testimonies, I sometimes wonder, *What do these words mean for those who suffer, for the teenager dying of cancer, for the parents receiving the news that their newborn child is severely brain-damaged, for the families of the twenty thousand people murdered in our country last year? What do these words about God's power communicate about the kind of God we worship, especially when often those speaking appear well dressed, well fed, and well off?* Clearly our understanding of God's power requires biblical revision.

Look closely at the resurrection figure of Jesus in the Gospels. Notice that he continues to bear in his resurrected body the wounds of crucifixion. I am reminded of an ancient legend that describes how the devil tried to enter heaven by pretending to be the risen Christ. Accompanied by his throng of demons disguised as angels of light, he stood at the gates of heaven shouting aloud, "Lift up your heads, O ye gates; and be ye lifted up, ye everlast-

ing doors; and the King of glory shall come in." The
angels of heaven responded with the refrain of the
psalm, "Who is this King of glory?" Then the devil
gave himself away. Opening his arms he answered,
"I am." In this act of arrogance he showed the
angels his outstretched hands. There were no nail-
prints. The angels of heaven refused to let him in.

Through those wounds written into his resurrected body, Jesus gives us an immeasurably rich
symbol for glimpsing the ever present power of
God's love. Plumbing its depths we see that suffering and evil are real; love often gets crucified
and people do get hurt. That is the nonnegotiable
reality of the world that we share. Nevertheless
(and that is a good resurrection word), the strong
love of God always has the final word. Nothing
can hold it back from working out its purposes.
Not only does the Holy One experience our suffering as though it was his own, he is also relent-
lessly seeking to bring light and life where there
seems to be only darkness and death. When this
happens for us, even in a small way, we experience a little Easter.

I recall a sudden reversal of all that I had hoped
for in a vocational sense. For almost ten years I
had cherished a dream of beginning a small missionary congregation within the inner city. After
years of exploration, however, it seemed best to

those in my church's hierarchy that permission not be granted for this endeavor. When I received the news it was a painful moment. I felt that I had reached a kind of vocational cul-de-sac. Slowly I realized that I needed to relinquish an image of myself as a radical pioneer in congregational renewal. Simultaneously with this letting-go there came a surprise opportunity for me to join a pastoral team that would give me space in which I could foster people's spirituality in individual and small-group settings. For the past three years this is what I have been doing, experiencing a real sense of fulfillment. Looking back now I see this new vocational beginning as a little Easter.

Perhaps you can testify to a little Easter. When courage is given for the despairing heart to keep living through the pain, that is a little Easter. When listening friendship enables the timid and withdrawn soul to slowly open up, that is a little Easter. When inner pain causes the self-reliant and self-sufficient to ask for help from beyond themselves, that is a little Easter. When a forgiving spirit empowers an oppressed people to reconcile with their oppressors for the sake of building a new nation, such as we have witnessed during our time of national transition in South Africa, that is a little Easter. Just about anytime we are surprised with new possibilities for life and healing in the midst of brokenness and decay, there is a little Easter that gives us a glimpse of the resurrection power of God's love made manifest in the crucified and risen Jesus.

Jesus is our picture of God. Filtering all our ideas about the Holy One through this decisive disclosure of himself in Jesus of Nazareth is the only safe way to redraw our God-picture. This is what I have been seeking to do ever since that surprising question in the office of my mentor and friend. I have come to learn that the God whose face I see in Jesus speaks to each one of us by name and whispers, "You are loved just as you are. I am Abba, your heavenly parent, who welcomes you with open arms when you come home to me. Your presence is deeply desired at the family table of my friendship. When you hurt my other children through your actions and words I get angry, though my anger will never stop me from loving you. On the cross I died so that you would know the full extent of my offer of forgiveness. Your suffering is my suffering. Your grief is my grief. In your darkness and pain I want you to know that I'm constantly seeking to bring about for you another little Easter. This is how much I love you."

When our hearts and minds are touched by this great love we are ready to explore the adventure of the spiritual life.

Following the Signpost Together

Each chapter will be followed by a set of questions for a group to explore together. These questions will assume that you have begun to search out your own personal responses to those issues raised in the chapter just read.

1. Write the word *God* on a sheet of newsprint. Brainstorm your immediate responses to this word. Record all these under the word *God.*

2. Share the major negative components of your present God-picture. Where were these learned in the past?

3. Michael Ramsay makes the statement that "God is Christlike and in him there is no un-Christlikeness at all." How do you respond to this comment?

4. What would it mean for you to begin re-drawing your picture of God? How would this affect your everyday way of life?

5. When did you first become aware of God's personal love for you?

Developing a Christian Memory

Seldom has one sentence imprinted itself so powerfully on my mind. Written by that remarkable rabbi, Abraham Joshua Heschel, the thirteen words have signposted the direction of my faith-journey ever since I first read them. As I have learned to follow this particular signpost, my awareness of the Holy One's active presence throughout my life has been considerably strengthened. The sentence reads: "Much of what the Bible demands can be comprised in one word, 'Remember.'"

But, do I hear you protest, why dwell on the past? Surely if we take the rabbi's words seriously we will avoid engaging the challenges that face us in the present moment. Is not remembering a time-wasting activity that actually limits responsible participation in the immediate business of everyday life? Is it not more important to forget the past, live in the present, and plan for the future? Surely there is little value in remembering what has already taken place.

A pastor friend of mine would strongly disagree. Recently over a cup of coffee he described for me an evening out with his wife. It was their seventh wedding anniversary and celebrating the occasion with an act of reckless generosity, he took his wife to a rather exclusive French restaurant. Lingering over their candlelight supper they were able to talk together, uninterruptedly and leisurely, for over three hours. Aware that their relationship had felt the strains of parenting three young children, lack of quality time together, and the demands of conflicting work schedules, I expressed the hope that it had been a renewing time for them both. My friend's response intrigued me. "Yes, we spent the evening remembering. Between the courses of our meal we shared memories of our relationship together, joyful and painful." And then pausing for a moment as if he was inwardly registering a freshly birthed awareness he continued, "And you know, it's been a long time since I have felt so grateful and close in my marriage."

Just over a week ago I shared in a somewhat similar experience with my father. Presently my dad is living out his final days in a nursing home many hundreds of miles from where I live with my family. For the past four years he has struggled with the devastating effects of Alzheimer's disease, including the loss of his memory. As I sat holding his hand at what could have been my last visit, my mind went back over the years and I began remembering some of the things he had done for me. I remembered the times he had come to watch me play rugby. I remembered how he would fan me to sleep on hot summer nights. I remembered how he would put his arm around my shoulder, even as an adult, and remind me of his daily prayers for me. Sitting there with him I felt the tears well up behind my eyes—tears of appreciation and profound gratitude. Even though he could not speak or recognize me I felt close and deeply connected with him.

Can you see what begins to happen when we take time to remember? All of us carry memories within our hearts and when they are remembered we embark on a mysterious journey. The past breathes again in such a way that the present is injected with new life. Previously hidden significance bursts into conscious awareness. We see more clearly what we could not see before. Locked-up feelings find their freedom and in their appropriate expression bring renewed vitality and aliveness. Our sense of who we are and to whom we belong is nourished and sustained. These are just a few of the deep things that happen when we look back on the way we have come.

Biblical writers would affirm this understanding of memory. Engraved into their hearts was the conviction that God had made his loving presence known in their own history. When curious Israelite children desired to know more about God they were seldom taught abstract precepts. Memories were shared with them. They were told stories of the Lord their God who had brought their parents out of Egypt, led them through the wilderness, made water flow from flint rock, fed them manna in the wilderness, and protected them from scorpions and poisonous snakes. For people of the covenant, remembering was no cop-out. Remembering God's loving presence active in their past made that presence real within the present. No wonder the answering prayer of the psalmist echoes with the cry: "I remember you, O Lord."

Christian faith likewise is grounded in remembrance. Students of early church history remind us that within the early Christian communities the first obligation of the apostle involved making the faithful remember what they had received. The new Christ-follower needed to develop a Christian memory. Such a memory found its primary focus in the story of Jesus. Entering into the memory of his words and deeds, dying and rising, they were led into the inexhaustible loving heart of that Holy Mystery who had enfolded their lives from their very beginnings. The command of Jesus in connection with the breaking of bread applied to the whole of their lives: "Do this in remembrance of me."

Remembering Jesus in the Gospels

Developing a Christian memory that is centered around Jesus requires personal engagement with the Gospels. Without them it would be nearly impossible for us to know Jesus, and, through him, the character and nature of God. This is why the Gospels are so very important. Reflecting on his reasons for recording the deeds of Jesus, Gospel-writer John explains, "But these are written so that you may come to believe that Jesus is the Messiah . . ." (John 20:31). Almost every line of his book, and those of Matthew, Mark, and Luke, has the power to lead its readers into an enriched relationship with Jesus, provided it is read with carefulness and a sense of expectant encounter. Knowing this to be true, spiritual guides throughout the centuries have encouraged Christ-followers to constantly meditate on the figure of Jesus as he is revealed in the Gospels.

I have sought to take this counsel seriously in my own pilgrimage and have often offered it to fellow pilgrims. Frequently in my work as a pastor I meet people who are hungry for a living spirituality, people who, while they may be tired of religion, yearn for a firsthand relationship with the Holy One that will empower their lives with a fresh sense of vision. Reflecting on my conversations with these seekers after God I've noticed a remarkable similarity in the yearnings expressed. How do I come to know God? How can I deepen my friendship with him? How does God want me to live my life together with him? Usually I respond with one phrase: *Keep company with Jesus in the Gospels.*

How do we go about doing this? Allow me to be quite practical and straightforward in my response. Choose one Gospel with which you would like to journey over the next year. If undecided about which one, I would suggest the shortest, the Gospel according to Mark. Most scholars agree that Mark's is the basic Gospel, preceding the other three. Set time aside, an hour or so, to read the Gospel through in one sitting. This will give you some sense of its overall continuity and predominant emphases. After you have done this, try on as regular a basis as possible to read a short passage from its pages. As you read, keep company with Jesus. Try to understand his feelings about God, notice the way he relates to people, listen to the message he brings, explore his views about material things, and watch what he does. Consider always what all this would mean for you if you were to live your life as Jesus would if he were in your place.

Establishing a basic habit of devotional Gospel reading fosters the formation of a Christian memory. As we follow Jesus through the pages of the Gospels we are reminded of what God is like and how we can live in partnership with him. The Holy Spirit acts on this memory, causing Jesus to become for us a living presence and making us mindful of his wishes for our daily lives. Thus, we can see that gradually developing a Christian memory around the person of Jesus, growing in relationship with God, and practicing everyday discipleship all go hand in hand. Joseph Girzone describes these links well when he writes, "That is why a precise understanding of Jesus is so important for us, so we can share His vision of God and His understanding of human nature and frame for ourselves our own relationship with God within the context of the rest of His creation."[1]

Remembering Our Personal Stories

Another dimension of Christian memory is the remembering of our own personal stories. This practice happens in the biblical faith that "in him we live and move and have our being" (Acts 17:28). Life is continuously lived in God's creative, loving presence. Our lives are never secular. They are sacred journeys in which God is constantly involved, always seeking to disclose his gracious word and passionate love. From our very beginnings our lives have been divinely enfolded. Such is the conviction expressed in the psalmist's cry of wonder: "For it was you who formed my inward parts; you knit me together in my mother's womb" (Ps. 139:13).

In the early stages of my Christ-following pilgrimage I did not fully realize this. My impression was that God had only become part of my life when I turned to him at the time of my conversion. But as my understanding of God slowly developed I recognized that the Holy One had been present throughout my life, continuously loving me and inviting me to accept his friendship. When this finally became clear I began remembering my own personal history with the specific purpose of discerning God's ever present participation within it. Now if asked to share my faith-story I would begin by speaking about my earliest memories of warmth and kindness. Through experiences like these God had been working in my life long before I first became aware of him. This is what Paul helps Timothy to grasp when he writes, "I am reminded of your sincere faith, a faith that lived first in your grandmother Lois and your mother Eunice and now, I am sure, lives in you" (2 Tim. 1:5).

Mary, mother of Jesus, mentors us in this task of remembering. Crammed into her life are the contrasting experiences of expectation and disappointment, ordinariness and upheaval, joy and fear. Growing up in the uncomplicated plainness of Palestinian village life, she falls in love with a young upright Jewish man, Joseph. Wedding arrangements are set in joyful motion. However, a sudden angelic visitation turns Mary's life upside down. If willing, she will bear a child who will be called Son of God. Her trembling consent throws the engagement into the trauma of mistrust and suspicion. Only a dream in the middle of the night restores to the relationship the commitment of Joseph.

Events surrounding the eventual divine birth are wearying and chaotic: traveling seventy miles on a donkey's back from Nazareth to Bethlehem, struggling vainly to locate a motel room for rest and renewal, giving birth in the messiness of a stable shed, receiving visits from poor shepherds and rich wise men bringing gifts of worship, hearing news of a hit squad's intention to kill all boys under the age of two. Hidden among these experiences there is a still moment, overlooked by many, but noticed by Luke. Without overstatement or exaggeration, the activity of this moment is recorded for us: "Mary remembered all these things and thought deeply about them" (Luke 2:19 TEV). Engaging faithfully in the ancient practice of her people, Mary is both the faithful Israelite and our symbol for the remembering life.

Meditating imaginatively on Mary's still moment yields important clues regarding a starting point for the remembering of our personal stories. Certainly the cold recall of the computer, the mechanical reproduction of the photographic mind, is not what she was about. Developing a Christian memory, an alternative translation of the above Lukan text implies, is a matter of the faith-soaked heart. We begin from a stance of faith. The Holy One has always been with us, even when we were unaware of his presence. Knowing this, we then recall significant experiences and reflect on them, pondering how God has been present within them.

One of the most practical ways of following Mary's example involves the writing of a spiritual autobiography. A lengthy book is not what I have in mind. Simply set aside a few hours spread over a period of several days. *Begin first by making a random list of those key moments in your life when the Holy One seemed particularly close,* moments when your life was touched by a sacred sense of awe and wonder and gratitude. Memories could range from a powerful awareness of life's utter giftedness, like witnessing the birth of a baby, to an answered prayer for yourself or a loved one. Limit your list to about ten such memories. Next to these experiences describe the feelings you had during them. Feelings of deep joy and wholeness are usually a sign of God's presence. Celebrate these experiences as sacraments of God's self-giving love especially shared with you.

Or you can begin by putting down on paper all that has been given over the years. As Paul reminds us, "What do you have that you did not receive?" (1 Cor. 4:7). Reflecting on your life journey, try to notice all the gifts that you have received. These would include people who have touched your life with kindness, opportunities for growth that have crossed your path, talents and abilities that have enriched your life and brought blessing to others. See in all these gifts the generous love of the One who is the giver of all good things. The Giver is present in the gift. When your list is completed, offer to God your heart's response of joyful gratitude and appreciation.

The second stage of one's spiritual autobiography relates to the pain that we have known. Not all memories are joyful. For six weeks in 1978, I had the privilege of sharing in the life of the Church of the Saviour, a small ecumenical congregation in inner-city Washington now finding expression through numerous faith-communities scattered throughout the city. I remember one lunch date with Gordon Cosby, the church's cofounder and pastor. Forty years of servant ministry had instilled in my lunch companion a profound pastoral wisdom. Together we were reflecting on the challenges of preaching within the contemporary urban context. "Never forget," he said thoughtfully, "each time you stand up to preach, each person in your congregation is sitting next to a pool of tears."

In our spiritual autobiographies how do we connect memories of painful suffering with the presence of God? I remember a dear friend and colleague asking this question some years ago. On a bleak winter's night, June 17, 1992, over forty unsuspecting inhabitants of Boipatong were brutally and senselessly murdered. Shock waves triggered by the massacre rippled throughout South Africa. The extent of the barbarism was horrendous: a heavily pregnant woman hacked to death, a nine-month-old baby stabbed, and a number of elderly persons mutilated beyond description. At the memorial service my friend preached. After recalling the events of that fateful night he pointed the worshipers to a gaunt, hollow-eyed figure

nailed to a cross, mouth wide open as if scream-
ing in agony, and said simply, "God weeps and suffers silently with you."

Each one of us sits beside a pool of tears. These
pools reflect those memories hard to bear. Whatever they are—childhood abuse, relationship
betrayal, parental neglect, unfair tragedy—these
memories are an integral part of our spiritual
autobiographies. Often we try to ignore these
wounds from the past. When probed in conversation they are painful and we say to each other,
"Let's talk about something more positive." But
painful memories pushed under the carpets of
our consciousness cripple our capacities to live
and love fully. "Forgetting the past," writes Henri
Nouwen, "is like turning our most intimate
teacher against us."[2]

Make notes, therefore, in your spiritual autobiography of memories of past pain. Pay particular attention to those feelings associated with
each painful memory. What my colleague did for
the Boipatong mourners we must do for ourselves. Gently connect the memories with the ever
present suffering love of the crucified and risen
Lord. Keep the cross before you. Commute for
however long seems appropriate between the
painful memory and the crucified Jesus. There is
always a cross in the anguished heart of God. Lit-

tle wonder Studdart Kennedy, the wartime chap-
lain known affectionately throughout Britain as
"Woodbine Willie," spoke of God as the greatest
sufferer of all, the One who shares our suffering
more than we can ever fully comprehend.

Recalling past pain can be quite traumatic.
Already we have noted that we spend a great deal
of energy avoiding inner pain. Eventually paying
attention to it could be overwhelming. Often
those we love the most, hurt us the most, and it is
usually extremely difficult facing these wounds.
Besides writing out the experiences of pain, it may
be necessary to find a professional person, like a
qualified counselor or therapist, to be a "wailing
wall." At different stages of our lives all of us need
a human wailing wall, a person who can sit with
us beside our pool of tears as an embodiment of
God's compassion and comfort.

This remembering of past pain takes place with
a hopeful heart. Christ, the crucified One who both
understands and shares our suffering, lives beyond
crucifixion. His living presence is constantly at
work in every painful memory from the past, seeking all the time to bring forth another little Easter.
This resurrection power of God's love cancels the
power of hurt memories to pronounce the final
word about our lives. Exposing our painful past to
the light of the risen Lord is therefore absolutely

crucial. Through the power of his crucified love Christ can bring healing for the wounded child within, can strengthen the betrayed heart to give itself away again, can restore confidence in the conquest of death. As the chorus line goes, "Because He lives I can face tomorrow."

The third stage involves writing down those ways in which God has used you to bring light and hope into the lives of others. For some this part of the spiritual autobiography could prove difficult to do. Some may feel they are being vain and conceited. Yet keeping track of positive things done for others can help one experience the joy of sharing in a living partnership with God. So ask the Lord to bring to mind moments when you have been a bearer of his loving presence. Write them down no matter how insignificant they may seem. Often the small gesture of love and kindness can carry a meaning far greater than what seems outwardly apparent. When your list is completed give thanks to God for the privilege of being his partner in his ongoing work in his world today.

Writing a spiritual autobiography is a holy experiment in remembering. Through our participation in this experiment our experience of the Holy One is immeasurably enriched. As we notice how God has been with us in the past, our present awareness of his companionship is deepened. As we discern those divine invitations that have been offered, our spirits are sensitized to God's initiatives as they come to us now. As we reflect on those times when God has used us, our willingness to risk ourselves in his service today is increased. Undoubtedly there exists an intimate connection between this kind of remembering and growing in an authentic spirituality.

Remembering the Present Day

Daily reflection constitutes one other crucial dimension of developing a Christian memory. Through its practice we keep our remembering up to date. No day is empty of God's presence. In the people we meet, the tasks we do, the difficulties we face—and in our responses to them—God is continually trying to catch our attention and give us fresh glimpses of his loving presence. Pausing for a few quiet moments before we fall asleep creates the space needed to reflect on how God has been with us over the past twelve hours or so, and how we have responded.

It was just over five years ago that I first began to practice a form of daily reflection. The doors had closed on my hoped-for vocational future and I needed to make some critical decisions. Not wanting to hurry into premature choices I decided to do the Spiritual Exercises of St. Ignatius within the context of my daily life. Finding my way to a little monastery in the backstreets of Johannesburg, I asked one of the monks if he would lead me through this program of biblically based, Christ-centered meditations. Very kindly he agreed. In our first interview together he spelled out the required time commitments. For the following nine-month period I would need to set aside an hour each morning before work for prayer around the Scriptures, and in the evening spend about ten minutes doing "an examen of consciousness." I had no idea what this strange sounding phrase meant. Patiently my newly found monk friend explained what this would involve. I can still remember the rough outline of his answer:

"Before you go to bed look over the day and see where you need to be thankful. Ask the Spirit of God to show you what he wants you to see. Ask him also to reveal where he has been present in your life throughout the day, either in you or in others, and what he has been asking of you. Reflect upon your moods during the day. See if there is any underlying attitude that needs conversion. Ask the Lord for forgiveness for those moments when you did not respond to his love. And in closing, think about the following day and ask God for whatever help and guidance you need."

For the following nine months I practiced the examen of consciousness. It became the highlight of the entire Ignatian adventure. More than anything else that I did during that time, it sharpened my sensitivity to the nudges and promptings of the Spirit. I began to discern where God was leading me. Since the completion of the exercises I have continued practicing the examen at the end of each day. It doesn't take longer than five to ten minutes and continues to keep me in tune with the presence and leading of God in different aspects of my everyday life. I have also learned that one can take the basic principles of the examen and apply them to any period of time—the preceding hour, day, week, or year. Indeed following the guidelines of the examen can become a built-in way of life.

In the pursuit of an authentic spirituality, words count for very little and practice means everything. Therefore you may want to experiment with the examen immediately. It will not take you longer than about ten minutes. Place yourself consciously in God's presence, asking for his light as you review the past few hours. Then ponder the following questions, which summarize the major emphases of the examen: What have I to be thankful for? What strong moods have I experienced and what attitudes lie beneath them? For what do I need to ask forgiveness? For what do I need God's help and guidance tomorrow? When you have completed this small experiment, you have just done your first examen of consciousness![3]

"Chosen before the world began" is a recurring biblical phrase to which I constantly return. It describes our earliest beginnings in the loving heart of God. There each of us knew the indescribable joy of being God's delight and desire. Imprinted on our hearts and buried beneath layers of consciousness is this primal memory. Remembering God's loving presence in Jesus Christ, in our own personal stories, and in our daily lives signposts the way toward that memory hidden in our hearts.

Following the Signpost Together

1. Go around the group and ask what have become known as the four "Quaker questions." Think back over your life during the ages of 7 and 11, and then share:

   • Where did you live during this time, and who were family for you?
   • How was your home heated?
   • Where did you look for personal warmth and affection?

- When was the first time in your life that God became more than a word?

2. Share *one* of your most significant spiritual experiences.
3. How have you experienced the presence of God in tough times?
4. Read as a group Psalm 139:1–18. Identify a phrase that strikes you in the light of your own experience of God over the years. Share this phrase and comment on its meaning for you.

Receiving the Kingdom

*I*t was a nerve-racking moment. I had resigned from secular employment and offered myself as a candidate for the ordained ministry. The first requirement involved passing an oral examination before the annual synod. Examining me was a bishop well known for his direct and stern approach. His first question seemed simple enough.

"Tell me, Mr. Hudson," asked the bishop, "what was the central message of Jesus?"

"Forgiveness of sins, sir!" I shot back immediately.

"No," responded the bishop, matter of factly.

"Peace on earth, sir," I tried again, remembering the line from the chorus of the heavenly host that startled sleepy shepherds in the middle of the night.

"No," said the bishop again, as my face, I'm sure, began to redden.

By this time I thought it would be best for me to give up trying and I said so. Leaning over his desk the bishop caught my eyes in his solid gaze and said, "I want you to never, never forget that the main message of Jesus was, 'the kingdom of God is at hand.'"

The bishop was right. While I had certainly described aspects of the kingdom, I had overlooked the key description used by Jesus to proclaim his message. Recall that dramatic curtain-opening moment of his public ministry when Jesus comes to Galilee. Almost thirty years of hidden preparation lay behind him. Eventually, as he emerges from his wilderness struggle with the devil, Jesus embarks on his life's work. Mark summarizes the essence of his inaugural sermon in one explosive phrase, "the kingdom of God is at hand" (Mark 1:15 KJV).

What do we make of this phrase? To begin with, our thinking about it must be shaped primarily by our picture of God. After all, it is his kingdom. Jesus, as we have seen, discloses God as an infinitely caring father who runs down the road and welcomes home a wayward child with a big hug. Then he showers some significant gifts on the boy, plans a party for him, and accepts him back into the family house. This is the nature of the King to whom the kingdom belongs. Therefore, whatever else it may be, the kingdom is wherever the loving will of the Father effectively reigns. It is an eternal kind of life characterized by the presence of grace and mercy and powerful little Easters.

Entering into its orbit, as that prodigal son did, is all about coming home to ourselves, being re-united with family, and learning to live again as a beloved daughter or son of the King.

Jesus is this kingdom on two legs. This is made clear in his response to his critics after he had delivered a person from the dark forces of evil. He answers them, "But if it is by the Spirit of God that I cast out demons, then the kingdom of God has come to you" (Matt. 12:28). Wherever Jesus ministered in word and deed the loving will of the Father effectively reigned. When he healed the sick, that was the kingdom of God. When he forgave sins, that was the kingdom of God. When he shared meals with the outcasts and outsiders of his day, that was the kingdom of God. Hence while God's kingdom has been in existence right from the very beginning of creation, in the person of Jesus it became clearly visible and was made available to all. Through him the kingdom of God was indeed at hand.

And it is at hand for us. We don't need to wait for the kingdom until we are dead. Our lives can be touched today by its resurrection power. We can begin learning immediately what it means to live within its presence. Like the earliest disciples we can experience its gradual transformation of our everyday lives. Like them we can discover how to bear its reality into those situations where it is seemingly absent. But first we must receive it. We cannot give to others what we do not possess. The good news is that through the crucified and risen Jesus present throughout the world, the kingdom is available as a sheer gift. "Do not be afraid, little flock," says Jesus, "for it is your Father's good pleasure to give you the kingdom" (Luke 12:32).

Clenched Fists or Open Hands

Gifts are received with open hands. It is the same with the offer of God's kingdom. Recently I reflected with a dear friend about her beginnings on the Christian Way. At the conclusion of a usual Sunday worship service the officiating pastor extended an invitation. All worshipers were asked to clench their hands into tightly balled fists. Evidently this was not unusual for this congregation. However, on this particular morning things seemed different for my friend. The liturgy came alive and she profoundly experienced a sense of God's searching love. She sat in the silence, clenched fists resting on her lap. Finally worshipers were invited, should it be their desire, to express their response to God by unclenching their fists. My friend described the moment simply:

"Somehow I stopped resisting and slowly opened my hands to God."

We live either with clenched fists or open hands. These radically opposed images symbolize two contrasting ways in which we can relate to the Holy One. Tightly closed hands indicate our refusal to be part of his kingdom of "righteousness and peace and joy in the Holy Spirit" (Rom. 14:17). Rather, we want to live our lives on our terms and according to our own wills. Clenched fists distance us from the intimacy and friendship that God desires to share with us. They suggest that we want to keep Christ outside of our lives where his transforming influence can be kept at arm's length. To put it bluntly, clenched fists say no to God and the gift of his kingdom.

Open hands say yes to God. Taking the hand stretched out toward us in Christ, open hands express our heart's desire to receive all that God longs to give. They make visible our inward willingness to let God be God in our lives and to let him lead and guide us. Hands opened in this way toward the Holy One are simultaneously opened to those around us. They speak of our willingness to be vulnerable, to give and to receive, to come home, and to be part of the family that is the kingdom of God. Open hands connect with friend and neighbor.

Only hands opened by repentance and belief can receive this gift of the kingdom. "The kingdom of God has come near," proclaims Jesus and so his listeners are urged to "repent, and believe in the good news" (Mark 1:15). Contained in this response are two frequently misunderstood verbs. Many associate "repent" with negative images of gloomy preachers threatening their listeners with grim warnings of pending doom. Meanwhile "believe," in the minds of some, has been tragically shrunk to mean mere intellectual assent to credal statements. And in this sense as John Wesley has reminded us, "the devil also believes in God." Both verbs must be reclaimed with their rich biblical meanings.

The Open Hand of Repentance

Repentance is the translation of a Greek word, *metanoia,* which essentially implies a change in our way of thinking. It does not mean putting ourselves down, being preoccupied with our sinfulness, or feeling sorry for ourselves. Neither is it aimed at earning acceptance, deserving forgiveness, or achieving God's favor. True repentance is something altogether different. It involves the complete reversal of our mind and outlook that turns us in a new direction, changes our distorted attitudes, and gives our lives a new center from which a new kind of life begins emerging. Allow me to unpack a little more of each of these three aspects belonging to true repentance.

Repentance turns us in a new direction. Mary's experience in the garden of the resurrection provides a striking picture of this truth. She is standing outside the tomb where the body of Jesus has been laid, obviously overcome by her grief. She is bewildered and desperate. The One who gave her back her life was killed. Ever since the events of that terrible Friday she has been living in darkness. While standing there in the garden she is joined by another. Initially she thinks that her companion is the gardener. And then the stranger speaks one simple word: "Mary." She recognizes the voice. It is that same voice that several months earlier assured her of her belovedness and worth. In describing her immediate response, Gospel-writer John gives us a beautiful picture of genuine repentance: "She turned toward him and cried out . . ." (John 20:16 NIV).

Meditate for a few moments on Mary's "turning moment." Notice that she turns as she is, in her grief and pain and tears. But it is a turning toward life. One of the central meanings of repentance is turning toward Jesus, as we are, and accepting the gifts of the kingdom that he freely offers us. Such turning is never a once-and-for-all experience. Conversion always continues. Hence repentance becomes a way of life—a life-long process of turning toward the Holy One that happens one day at a time. Anthony, the well-known desert-father from the fourth century, is reported to have once said, "Every morning again I say to myself, today I start."

Repentance changes our distorted attitudes. Attitudes are the way we perceive reality. They exercise a profound influence on the way we live our lives and respond toward others. Over the years we acquire literally hundreds of different attitudes, many of which block us from living free and joyful lives. Turning toward Jesus allows him the opportunity to change those attitudes that are diseased. Over time he imparts to us a new vision and fresh understanding of our lives. Joseph Girzone spells out these changes of attitude and perception in fuller detail: "We think differently about God. We think differently about material things. We think differently about ourselves and others. We think differently about rich people and poor people. We see God's creation and everything in it as sacred. Given the time God will eventually transform our whole life."[1]

One of the first changes that God brought about in my own life was in my attitude toward words. Before turning to Christ, words were not that important to me. Often I would use them casually and without much thought. Gently God seemed to impress on my mind that words were more than words. I began to think differently about them. I began to see them as carriers of life and light as well as death and darkness. To this day this change continues— learning to see words as one of the most important ways in which we can share in the ministry of the kingdom.

Repentance gives our lives a new center from which a new kind of life begins emerging. From early childhood onward our lives are dominated by an assumption that "I am at the center of the universe and everything else must revolve around my wishes, my desires, my interests, and my needs." We become imprisoned in this cell of self-centeredness and are unable in our own strength to break free. The consequences of our selfishness reveal themselves all around us. Consider how self-centered behavior prevents the giving of ourselves, sabotages intimate relationships, and ruins the life of those groups to which we belong. Reflect on how the social consequences of this assumption work themselves out in the structural evils of our time. South Africa has been the painful context for my learning in this regard. The essence of apartheid, the legacy of which we are presently seeking to untangle ourselves as a nation, was legalized self-interest. Its consequences bankrupted the soul of a nation.

When we are given a glimpse of the possibilities of what our lives could become if they were part of the kingdom, we reconsider the center of our lives. With theologian William Temple we realize that there "is only one Sin, and it is characteristic of the whole world. It is the self will which prefers 'my' way to God's—which puts 'me' in the center where only God is [should be] in place."[2] Facing this truth and accepting it as accurately describing our lives brings us to repentance. Turning toward the Holy One, we are able to slip over into a new center and enter on a new way of life. Not only are we born again, we begin to live again.

Establishing this new personal center does not happen without struggle. When we put God at the hub of our lives, we find ourselves exposed to the blazing light of his self-giving love. Touched by these rays we see more clearly the dark and hidden depths of our self-centeredness. We realize how much this sin-condition has permeated our past actions and behaviors. And we see how much it has hurt others— especially those closest to us. While these insights make us more conscious of just how much God really forgives us, they also, if our repentance is to be real, lead us to want to make amends so far as we can. This process demands courage and wisdom.

Neither is repentance a quick fix. We do not become new people overnight. Indeed turning toward Christ introduces into our lives a new inner battle. I discovered this very soon after my initial conversion moment. There was, I learned, a deeply ingrained part of me that still wanted to be at the center, to be in control, to do it my way. Then there was also that part of me that really wanted to live from my new center in God. This battle continues to rage to this day. Camouflaged amid a variety of self-centered attitudes and behaviors my sin-condition continues trying to regain the upper hand over my life. Its disguises range from impatience in traffic snarlups and withdrawal when my needs are not met to sometimes presumptuously believing that I can meet everyone else's needs without giving time to my own. Often I lose the battle and get discouraged. But I'm learning to gently return to Christ who never leaves me, open my life again to his gifts of acceptance and mercy, confess my failures, and continue on the way. Repentance, in other words, is becoming a way of life that keeps me open to grace.

The Open Hand of Belief

Belief opens the other hand to receive God's gift of the kingdom. To believe, in the New Testament sense of the word, involves clear content, risky surrender, and persistent effort. It means affirming something very particular about Jesus, entrusting ourselves to him, and steadfastly learning from him how to live. Holding these components of believing together in creative tension keeps Christian belief from deteriorating into sheer fuzziness. I want therefore very carefully to tease out what is meant by each of these interwoven threads.

To believe means affirming something very particular about Jesus. For almost twenty-five years I have wrestled with Jesus' question, "Who do you say that I am?" During this time I have frequently sought to keep company with Jesus in the Gospels. I have come to see Jesus as the most alive, aware, and responsive human being that ever lived. I have come to recognize his dying as revealing love's response in the face of evil. I have come to realize that something most extraordinary must have taken place after the crucifixion in order to transform those frightened and grieving disciples into bold witnesses willing to die for their beliefs. I have found it most reasonable to accept the biblical explanation accounting for this transformation—that this man Jesus was both fully human and God come in the flesh, was tortured and killed, was resurrected from death, and is among us now in the power of his Spirit, making available God's gracious kingdom as he did for his earliest disciples.

When we talk about believing in Jesus there is certain content to it. Believing in him we come to believe particular things about him. This was the experience of the early disciples in the New Testament and, as I have tried to illustrate from my own pilgrimage, can be our experience today. As these men lived in the company of Jesus they came to understand him in a particular way. From their Old Testament heritage they were able to find words to describe this understanding. New Testament scholar Donald English points out that Jesus was someone about whom they were able to say: Son of Man, Lord, Savior, Emmanuel, Word of Life.[3] These titles were all ways through which the disciples could affirm their bottom-line belief—the belief that in Jesus, God had stepped into human history. Or as Jesus himself put it, "Whoever has seen me has seen the Father. . . . Do you not believe that I am in the Father and the Father is in me?" (John 14:9–10).

To believe involves entrusting ourselves to the crucified and risen Christ. I have learned most about this experience of surrender through friends recovering from alcohol abuse. I remember the testimony of a middle-aged father and husband. Celebrating his tenth anniversary of sobriety and sanity he recounted the painful devastation his drinking habits had caused. A hushed congregation listened intently as he described his personal history of denial and delusion, of how he had arrogantly assumed that he could be the center of his own life. Gesturing toward the candlelit altar on which stood a stark wooden cross, his concluding words revealed the radical and ongoing process of real trusting.

"Ten years ago I found myself at the end of my rope. At an evening service in this church I came forward and knelt there at the altar and looked long and hard at that cross. I said to God, 'I've tried to take your place in my life and have made a total mess. I ask for your forgiveness and surrender myself and my future to you. Show me how to live with you at the center.' And I've prayed these words almost every day since."

This testimony reveals the intimate links between repentance and belief. These two hands open together to receive the gift of the kingdom. If repentance turns our eyes toward the Holy One, believing relinquishes our lives into his loving hands. If repentance transforms our distorted attitudes, believing trusts that it is God who is at work. If repentance gives a new center to our lives, believing surrenders the old and yields ourselves to Christ who now becomes our Lord. And like repentance, entrusting ourselves to God in these ways is never a one-time experience. Shifting from a self-centered lifestyle into a God-centered way of life takes a lifetime.

I do not find it easy to believe like this, you may be saying under your breath. Do not force yourself. You are not alone in your struggle. It is not easy to entrust ourselves to God. Genuine belief seldom comes quickly or without struggle. We *learn* to trust God. Over the years I have been encouraged in this learning process by developing a maturer Christian memory, honestly facing my inability to overcome my sin-condition on my own, and simply asking God to help me trust him. When I am able to recognize that God is like Jesus, that his kingdom is truly available, and that he is able to do in my life what I cannot, there is released within me a fresh capacity to surrender myself into his hands.

To believe means steadfastly learning from Jesus how to live. Entrusting ourselves to him, we believe that he, more than anyone else who has ever lived, knows how to live. To believe in Jesus involves, therefore, learning how to live our lives in the kingdom as he did when he walked the roads of Palestine. This does not mean trying to copy the historical life of Jesus. That would lead us into the most deadly forms of legalism. Rather it means committing ourselves to Christ, immersing ourselves in his example and teaching as it comes to us in the four Gospels and learning from him how to put into practice what we see there. We do not attempt this while relying on our own strength. Our commitment, Jesus has promised us, will bring his constant presence into our everyday lives as a living and tangible reality. "Those who love me will keep my word, and my Father will love them, and we will come to them and make our home with them" (John 14:23). How we can begin on this way will be explored in coming chapters.

Opening Clenched Fists

As you end this chapter I invite you to share in a brief exercise. Wherever you may be sitting right now, make yourself comfortable and place both your hands on your lap. Curl up your fingers into tightly closed fists. Imagine that in these tightly clenched hands you are holding onto everything that is important to you—your life, your loved ones, your work, your possessions, your hopes and dreams for the future. Feel the tension build up from your hands and spread throughout your body. Now hear the words of Christ as if they were coming from a deep place within you: "The kingdom of God is available, repent and believe the good news." As you are able, allow your response to find expression in the slow opening of your hands.

May you know the joy of receiving the kingdom!

Following the Signpost Together

1. Write the phrase *The kingdom of God* on a sheet of newsprint. Brainstorm your understandings of this phrase and write them down.
2. Have you ever opened your hands to the gift of the kingdom? How did this first take place in your life?
3. Share one change that God seems to have brought about in your life since you first turned toward him.
4. Share one way in which the sin-condition manifests itself in your present way of life.
5. What has helped you to entrust yourself more deeply to Christ?

The group may wish to end its discussion by sharing together in the exercise outlined at the close of the chapter.

Acknowledging Our Shadow Selves

ust as I am . . . O Lamb of God, I come."
These words from the old evangelical
hymn accompanied my first ever public
commitment to Jesus. They echoed my
heartfelt yearning to yield myself completely to the
One who had given his life for the world. Yet I am
aware today, however earnest and well-meaning
that desire was, how little of myself that night I
actually surrendered to God. I realize now that as
I walked forward to the altar I was only taking my
first conscious step along an unending spiritual
journey that we call conversion.

Conversion is a continuing process that unfolds
one day at a time as we bring more and more of
ourselves to God. "Once converted, fully converted," is a deceptive slogan. It suggests that conversion is a destination where we arrive rather
than a road along which we journey. Getting to
know who we are, especially those more hidden
aspects of our personalities, and consciously yield-
ing ourselves to the God who unconditionally

accepts us in Christ signposts our way along this conversion road. Someone once put it thus: "Conversion is the surrender of as much of myself as I know today to as much of Christ as I know today."

Several years ago I was introduced to a concept that opened up new possibilities for deeper self-understanding. During my visit in 1978 with the Church of the Saviour in Washington I visited the Potter's House, their coffee and book shop, in the multiethnic Adams Morgan area. There I stumbled across a small book that was to become a treasured companion on my future journey along the conversion road: *Our Many Selves.* The title of the book is also a description of this concept. In her book Elizabeth O'Connor suggests that the human being tends to be not one unified self but a multitude of selves. In the opening lines of her book she describes the beginnings of her discovery in this regard. She writes, "It was during a time of painful conflict that I first began to experience myself as more than one. It was as though I sat in the midst of many selves. Some urged me down one path and some another. Each presented a different claim and no self gave another self an opportunity to be fully heard."[1]

When I first read these words they struck a deep responsive chord. While the author's language was unfamiliar, the experience described was not foreign. Especially in moments of decision making

and stress I have often felt myself pulled in oppos-
ing directions by the different parts of myself. Like
the experience shared by Elizabeth O'Connor
some would suggest that I follow one route, and
some another. Since my introduction to this concept I have sought greater understanding of the
many selves that make up my internal household.
Sometimes when faced with a decision, I imagine
them gathering together, each of them competing
for their own advantage. Naming these many selves
has made possible the needed distance to observe
them, listen to their stories, and so allow them to
extend my knowledge of who I am. There is the
cautious self, the gypsy self, the playful self, the
competitive self, the pleasing self, the caring self,
and others, some of whom I'm still getting to know.

Within conventional Christian circles there is a
widespread tendency to acknowledge only the
acceptable selves. Those considered unacceptable
are usually either neglected or rejected. This way of
denial, as we shall see later, has destructive consequences. Most tragic of all is that large tracts of our
inner life are prevented from experiencing God's
transforming friendship. Conversion can only continue as we acknowledge these shadow selves and
expose them to the light of God's love. There God is
able to embrace them with his grace, gather them
together around himself, and slowly weave them

into the new person that he is making. In this way
we collaborate with the Holy One in the ongoing
transformation of our lives. Using the language of
Paul the apostle: we begin to "work out [our] salva-
tion with fear and trembling" (Phil. 2:12 NIV).

Jesus' parable about the banquet meal provides
another way of describing the conversion process.
According to Jesus, his Father's kingdom is like a
joyful and festive dinner for which invitations are
sent out. Symbolizing the good news that the kingdom's doors are wide open, these invitations could
well have been worded, "You are loved, accepted,
and forgiven. The banquet has been prepared and
is ready now. Come and share in the feast. R.S.V.P.
Jesus of Nazareth." As the parable unfolds we notice
that the concerns of real estate, work, and family
give rise to empty excuses. The host then commands his servants, "Go out quickly into the streets
and alleys of the town, and bring me the poor, the
crippled, the blind, and the lame" (Luke 14:21 NEB).

Parables throb with many levels of meaning.
There is always more than we can explain. Certainly this is true about this parable. On the one
hand it has crucial social and corporate meanings.
It affirms the Holy One's all-inclusive love with its
distinctive bias toward those who suffer, challenges
us to extend hospitality to the marginalized, and
promotes the kingdom vision that social structures

reflect a special concern for the most vulnerable. On the other hand it contains a clear inner meaning. Elsewhere Jesus states that the kingdom is also within us (Luke 17:21). The divine host presides over the banquet at the deep center of our beings. Applied inwardly the parable invites us to search out the poor, crippled, blind, and lame aspects of our own inner lives and bring them into the banqueting chamber. Here the living Christ receives them with open arms and begins to include them in the new person that he is patiently forming.

Denying our shadow selves access to the banquet hinders our ongoing conversion, splits our lives dangerously, and renders us vulnerable to what we have denied. Peter, disciple of Jesus, is our teacher in this regard. Recall that dark night of our Lord's betrayal. Listen again to Peter's fervent affirmation of faith, "Lord, I am ready to go with you to prison and to death." This is Peter's courageous self speaking. Jesus, however, discerns beneath those bold words the presence of Peter's fearful, cowardly, and faithless selves. "I tell you, Peter, the cock will not crow this day, until you have denied three times that you know me" (Luke 22:33–34). But Peter will not face himself. Because Peter refuses to acknowledge these shadow selves, they eventually trip him up and find expression in actions of deceit, cowardice, and betrayal.

You see what has taken place in Peter's inner depth. Denying his shadow selves he is overcome by them. The biblical story here reinforces the psychological insight that we often become victims of what we inwardly deny. When unacceptable aspects of our personalities are denied they do not disappear. Instead they get pushed down into the basements of our personal lives from which they instigate much more havoc than they could ever cause if they were openly acknowledged. Acknowledging our many selves, especially those that prefer the shadows, is therefore absolutely crucial. Had Simon Peter heeded the prognosis of his soul that Jesus offered, acknowledged the presence of his shadow selves, turned to Christ and his friends for help, he may well have demonstrated the courage of a bold faithfulness.

Certainly this is what a courageous woman, giving her life away in sacrificial servanthood among refugees, is discovering. Whenever the opportunity presents itself we get together and reflect on the struggles and joys of her personal walk with Christ. Once she shared her discomfort regarding some dark emotions that she was experiencing. Her ministry among the impoverished seemed to be leading her into the brokenness of her own heart. She felt accused by these emotions and those aspects of her personality that they represented, and questioned her suitability for her work. I reminded her of the banqueting parable and drew her attention to its inner significance.

"But what do you suggest I actually do?" she asked, looking a little puzzled. "Next time you pray," I answered, "imagine Christ hosting a party banquet in your honor and inviting your presence. Befriend your resentful self and your angry self and bring them to the feast. Watch Christ welcome them and minister to them. You may want also to become better acquainted with these parts of your personality yourself."

A few weeks later our paths crossed again. I sensed a greater freedom in my friend and a renewed commitment to her ministry. I inquired about the source of this obviously newly found energy. Her answer came with a smile, "I've been enjoying some very good parties!"

Acknowledging our shadow selves is a vital prerequisite for traveling along the conversion road of the kingdom. It raises the practical question: How does one intentionally embark on this inner exploration in a life-giving way? Or to phrase it differently, How can we bring about a creative dialogue between Christ and the poor and crippled parts of our personality? Before I outline three practical ways of getting started on this journey I invite you to answer the following questions:

1. Have you ever said something to another person and then wished you could have somehow taken the words back?

2. Have you ever said something you didn't intend to say?

3. Have you ever done something you had no intention of doing?

4. Have you ever heard yourself say, "I just don't know what came over me; I just wasn't myself"?

5. Has anyone ever said to you, "You sure weren't your usual self"?

6. Has your spouse or a close friend ever said to you, "What got into you?"

7. Have you ever been shocked or frightened by thoughts that passed through your mind? Have you ever wondered where they come from?

8. Have you ever found yourself identifying with the "bad guy" in a movie or play? rooting for the villain? hoping the crook gets away?

9. Have you ever been caught up in watching a sports event and heard yourself shouting vengeful, even bloodthirsty, statements?

10. Have you ever wanted to "wipe out" a reckless driver, a manipulative coworker, or a nonstop talker?

11. Have you ever been introduced to someone and then later said to yourself, "I don't know why, but I just don't like that person"?

12. Have you ever realized that you have condemned another person for doing something that you also do but justify in yourself?
13. Have you ever caught yourself daydreaming about performing unrighteous acts?
14. Have you ever blamed someone else for what you knew was your fault?
15. Do you have any prejudices against anyone?

As author-counselor William Miller, who put this questionnaire together, writes, "I hope you answered yes to many of the questions in the Quick Quiz. If you did, it's a good indication that you are normal. It also indicates that you are at least *acquainted* with your 'shadow self,' that dark, hidden counterpart to the image you daily present to society."[2] In order to deepen your acquaintance with your shadow selves, you may find it helpful to experiment with the following menu of possibilities.

Pay Attention to Your Instant Reactions

Throughout the day we are bombarded with a wide variety of stimuli to which we are constantly reacting. These reactions seldom tell lies about our inner condition. They can also reveal aspects of our shadow selves that otherwise would remain altogether hidden. As such they provide the raw mate-

rial for God's continuing work of conversion in our
lives. Observing these reactions, listening to their
stories, and bringing them into the transforming
friendship offered by Christ facilitates this conversion. No one else can do this work of self-observa-
tion for us. Each of us has to do his or her own inner
work. Perhaps this is why Paul instructs Timothy,
"Pay close attention to yourself" (1 Tim. 4:16).

What happens, for example, when you are told
of another person's success in your own area of
work? Does the news instantly evoke a response
of joy on this person's behalf or does it produce
within you a note of jealousy? What happens when
you hear a colleague being praised for his efforts?
Are you able to freely share in this affirmation or
do you hear yourself saying something obviously
designed to underplay what has been achieved?
What happens at a four-way stop when it's your
turn to go, and the driver on your left races across
your path with a smirk on his face? Are you able to
let it be, or is your immediate reaction a curse that
you would never use in public? Paying attention
to these kinds of everyday reactions lays the foundation for your conversion to continue.

You may want to try the following experiment,
which I have adapted from the writings of Elizabeth O'Connor.[3] For the next forty-eight hours pay
attention to your instant reactions, especially those

that give you a negative way of feeling and respond-ing to events in life. Allow these reactions to intro-duce you to your shadow selves whoever they may be. These may be selves that lie or twist the truth, selves that get resentful when asked to help or that get irritable and frustrated when life does not work out the way they wanted. These may be selves that have the capacity for great violence or selves that are highly critical or overly defensive when criti-cism comes their way. Remembering the parable of the banquet, search these selves out and try to assume a shepherding attitude toward them. Befriend them and when you have some time available try to get to know them. You may find the following questions helpful. What sparked off their reaction? What are their yearnings? What is the aim of each? What are the things that nourish and keep these negative selves alive? Close off this time of self-exploration and dialogue by offering these shadow selves to Christ, the host of the banquet.

Find in Yourself
What You Condemn in Others

In biblical language, acknowledge the logs in your own eyes rather than focusing on the splin-ters in the eyes of others. Listen again to the teach-ing of Jesus in this regard: "Why do you see the speck in your neighbor's eye, but do not notice the log in your own eye? Or how can you say to your neighbor, 'Let me take the speck out of your eye,' while the log is in your own eye? You hypocrite, first take the log out of your own eye, and then you will see clearly to take the speck out of your neighbor's eye" (Matt. 7:3–5).

New Testament scholar Walter Wink has pointed out that we have in these words the earliest known teaching on projection. Projection operates on a deeply ingrained human tendency to see in others what we refuse to face in ourselves. The splinter we perceive so readily in the other's eye comes from that log occupying our own. While we often project our own darkness on those closest to us, we more frequently project our shadow selves on those people and organizations that we don't like. Indeed our enemies can help us see aspects of ourselves that we cannot discover any other way. Walter Wink writes, "We cannot come to terms with our shadow except through our enemies, for we have almost no other access to those unacceptable parts of ourselves that need redeeming except through the mirror that our enemies hold up to us."[4]

I learned this painful lesson attending a workshop during the mid-eighties. We were invited to write down the name of an enemy and to list all the things we disliked about this person or organization. I wrote down the name of the official security apparatus operating at that dark time in our nation's history. At its hands many personal friends and colleagues in ministry had been detained and tortured. My list of hated characteristics was lengthy. When asked to honestly consider what percentage of these listed characteristics were true of our own lives, I became very uncomfortable. My answer was 60 percent. For the sake of my own continuing conversion I knew I needed to own these personal logs, accept their reality in my own life, and bring them repeatedly into the presence of the banquet's host.

You may also find this exercise helpful. Make a note of those people you cannot stand. Write down those things that you intensely dislike about them—habits, beliefs, attitudes, behavior, traits, and so on. Consider that these may be splinters coming from logs in your own eyes. This list could help you in coming face-to-face with your own shadow selves. Remember the good news about our enemies—they help us recognize aspects of our personalities that otherwise we may never come to acknowledge. End this exercise by befriending your shadow selves and bringing them to the banquet. Ask the risen Christ to help you live with these parts of your life in a creative and life-giving way.

Step Imaginatively into a Gospel Story

Gospel stories are those told about Jesus and by him. They have a wonderful way of introducing us to God's transforming friendship and to our own hidden depths. Drawing us into an engagement with the crucified and risen Christ that goes beyond the intellectual, they shed light on our many selves and expose them to the converting action of the Spirit. I agree wholeheartedly with Morton Kelsey's evaluation when he writes, "The importance of the Bible's stories for constant transformation and renewal of human beings can hardly be overemphasized."[5]

Imagination enables us to step into the invisible world of the kingdom. I discovered this early in my own Christ-following pilgrimage. Before going to sleep I would imagine the risen Jesus sitting at the side of my bed, the blazing light of his love shining through the darkness. Then I would share aloud with him my deepest secrets, my joys, my struggles, and my hopes. In the silence afterward I would wait for his whisper in my thoughts and feelings. For many years this constituted my prayer-relationship with Christ. Gradually his presence became more real and tangible throughout my everyday life. Reflecting now on these beginnings I see the importance of using our imagination within our relationship with the Holy One. It is a

God-given faculty through which we can encounter Christ, or better still, through which Christ
can encounter us. Of course the image imagined
is not the reality (the word for this abuse is idola-
try); the image simply deepens our participation
in the reality it seeks to describe.

Now we can see how applying the imagination
to gospel stories enhances our experience of God's
transforming love. The practice, itself an ancient
one, is straightforward but requires time and effort.
Decide on a gospel story. Find a quiet place where
interruption is unlikely. Read through the story
slowly and prayerfully until it begins to live within
you. Become a participant in the story. Identify
yourself with one of the biblical characters present
in the gospel drama. Allow this person to represent
one of your many selves. For example, if you were
reading the story where Simon the Pharisee throws
a party for Jesus, you could identify yourself with
one or both of the key characters. A part of you may
be like Simon—objective, detached, and proper; on
the other hand, a part of you may be like the
woman—passionate, emotional, and generously
self-giving. Allow this person to express before the
Lord some of your thoughts, desires, and feelings.
Engage yourself with Christ who is the same yesterday, today, and tomorrow. Remember the aim of
the entire exercise is to facilitate an encounter

between you and Christ in the present. As you imaginatively experience the particular way your gospel character is encountered by Christ, you experience that part of your life that the character represents being loved in a similar way. You can spend a week, perhaps longer, with a gospel story in this way. The important thing is that you allow yourself to be encountered by the risen Lord as you are.

Recently I spent a morning leading a retreat with a group of young adults, most of whom were unable to read. I arranged in a circle a number of drawings, taken from Jean Vanier's beautifully illustrated *I Meet Jesus,* each of which depicts a gospel encounter. Inviting the retreatants to slowly walk around the drawings, I suggested they pick up one to which they felt inwardly attracted. The instructions for the morning were straightforward. "Go into the silence with the picture you have chosen. Spend some time just looking at it. Bring the scene to life with your imagination. Imagine that you are also there. Become whoever you want in the story. Receive the ministry of Christ. Talk with him about whatever happens." At the end of the morning we gathered together and shared our experiences. Listening to the personal sharing of one young man, I was again struck by the way God uses gospel stories as a means of self-discovery and growth. He said excitedly, "I came here to meet Jesus and I also met myself."

We are invited to a homecoming banquet. From the banqueting table the risen Christ offers to us with wounded hands broken bread and poured out wine. Tasting these gifts of God's acceptance we begin to accept ourselves. No part of our personality is excluded from the table. Acknowledging our shadow selves, befriending them with the friendship of Christ, and bringing them to the banqueting table continues our conversion. We are on the way toward becoming the person God wants us to be.

Following the Signpost Together

1. How do you understand conversion?
2. In what ways does the concept of "our many selves" correspond with your own experience?
3. Share your results from the Quick Quiz.
4. What have you discovered about yourself through paying attention to your instant reactions?
5. Share one part of your life that you need to befriend and bring to the banquet.

Belonging to the Family of God

We cannot be Christ-followers alone. This becomes clear from the moment we decide to follow Jesus along the conversion road. When we open our lives to him, he enters with arms around his brothers and sisters. Uncurling our clenched fists to receive the kingdom's gifts, we find they are touched by the hands of others. Without exception we discover ourselves situated among a new family, the family of God.

This was my experience from the earliest beginnings of my conscious relationship with Christ. Without others it is doubtful whether I would have ever even started on the Christ-following journey, let alone remained on it. It was a friend who first introduced me to Jesus and his message, within a gathered community of worshipers where I made my initial public commitment, and among a local congregation where I was nurtured in my new faith. And it was through the pages of an ancient book authored by fellow pilgrims thousands of years ago that I received guidance for the Way ahead. Saying yes to Jesus, I discovered, involved saying yes to his family, both visible and invisible.

Clearly the climate for growth and deepening in discipleship is community. We cannot become the persons God wants us to be without experiencing divine and human relationship. Genuine repentance and belief in Christ almost always immerses disciples into a life together. As we shall explore later, this belonging occurs at three basic levels: with those who have entered into the fuller life of the kingdom beyond death, among brothers and sisters of Jesus still present, and within personal friendships with particular fellow pilgrims on the way. Experiencing our belonging at each level is vital for a full Christ-following life.

Not everyone celebrates this given belonging. Some years ago, emblazoned across the T-shirt of a young woman pictured on *Time* magazine's front cover, were words that echoed a widespread disenchantment. "Jesus yes," the slogan shouted, "the church no." Asked about the meaning church has for her, a high profile South African activist responds, "It tends to contain and limit my quest for wholeness, rather than liberating me from myself and freeing me to be a better person."[1] Only yesterday I listened to an absent church member's angry accusation: "The church doesn't care."

Underlying these critical comments are understandable sentiments. Those with whom we are brought together are not always nice people. Reflected in their lives are self-centered attitudes and behaviors with which we all struggle. When personally disillusioned I remind myself that the main problem of the church is that people are often like me. Instead of consoling, understanding, and loving those around us we demand to be consoled, understood, and loved. The sin-condition is universal. Paul the apostle writes, "For there is no distinction, since all have sinned and fall short of the glory of God" (Rom. 3:22–23).

However, we cannot tear asunder Christ and his family. The kingdom of God is never a private banquet. Deciding to follow Christ locates us among fellow followers. Replay leisurely that curtain-opening moment in the ministry of Jesus beside the Sea of Galilee. Immediately on proclaiming the kingdom's availability, Jesus invites Simon and Andrew into discipleship. Leaving their nets they follow Jesus into an unchosen network of human relationships. Before long their lives are interwoven with James and John, whom Jesus has also called (Mark 1:16–20). Christ-following, these disciples would testify, is anchored in community.

This relational reality shaped significantly the convictions of the infant New Testament congregations. In the company of Jesus their leaders experienced with each other a depth of fellowship they had not known before. Their life together provided those nutrients necessary for personal transformation and growth in generous loving. They were convinced that the ongoing creation of similar community would be an indispensable goal for their ministry efforts. Confirming this conviction in the opening lines of his pastoral letter John exclaims, "We proclaim to you what we have seen and heard, so that you also may have fellowship with us. And our fellowship is with the Father and with his Son, Jesus Christ" (1 John 1:3 NIV).

Now we can understand why we read little in the New Testament about individual spiritual formation. The biblical language for growing in Christ is interdependent language. Gospel life is life together. Affirming this interdependence in our growth into wholeness is the recurring scriptural phrase "one another." Repeatedly we are encouraged to accept one another, serve one another, bear one another's burdens, care for one another.[2] Within community God is known, Christ takes shape, and the Spirit burns with transforming power. Within community we gradually become the people God wants us to be.

Authentic faith therefore intentionally integrates the Christ-follower into community.

Pause for a few moments and ask yourself: What are my feelings about being placed among fellow disciples? How seriously have I invested myself in this family whose foundation is Abba's all-inclusive, self-giving love in Jesus? What are my plans for a greater sharing in God's household? Indeed, how am I going to make real my belonging within the community of faith at the three levels mentioned above? Such integration occurs in three primary ways: connecting with those departed family members who form part of the "great cloud of witnesses," participating within the group life of the local congregation, and building faithful friendships with fellow pilgrim companions. Each requires fuller description, careful planning, and personal practice.

Connecting with the Great Cloud of Witnesses

Fellow African pilgrims constantly affirm the eternal dimensions of community. Mmutlanyane Mogoba, ex-prisoner of Robben Island and presently a deeply respected leader within the South African church, explains: "The departed person in Africa is not dead and removed from this life, but rather continues to be consciously affirmed in the family as the values, wisdom, and example of that person are incorporated into the family. The African is thus able to understand the Bible in a manner that westernized people never will. . . . We understand the reality of a person being surrounded by a great cloud of witnesses who have lived and departed this world."[3]

In those faith empowering opening lines of his twelfth chapter the writer to the Hebrews exclaims: "Therefore since we are surrounded by so great a cloud of witnesses . . . let us run with perseverance the race that is set before us" (Heb. 12:1). Nowadays scant attention is given to these unseen companions seeking to encourage us along the way. Disconnection characterizes our links with departed Christ-followers. Restricting the experience of God's community to the present day costs us dearly. It estranges us from our spiritual inheritance, promotes tunnel-vision discipleship, and shrivels up the soul. Witness the thirst among many contemporary Christ-followers for a richer, more-expansive, life-giving relationship with the living God.

A legendary story encourages a vital connection with our ancestors in the faith. Once upon a time the water of life, seeking to make itself known on the face of the earth, bubbled up in an artesian well and began to flow freely and strongly. The thirsty thronged to the well and drank gratefully

its life-giving water. However, it was not long before decisions were made to fence the well, charge
entrance fees, and make elaborate laws as to who
could come to the well. Soon the well was the protected property of the elite and powerful. Angry
and offended by these decisions the water
stopped flowing and began to bubble up elsewhere. Those who owned the first well were so
consumed by bureaucracy and legislative paper-
work they did not notice that the water had gone
elsewhere. They continued selling nonexistent
water and few people noticed that its life-giving
power was gone. Sadly the same fate overtook the
new artesian well. Again the water of life sought
another place—and this process has been going
on repeatedly throughout recorded history.

Discerning those past places and people where
the water of God's Spirit has brought nourishment
invigorates our own lives. This is not an exercise in
nostalgia. Neither do we worship our ancestors.
It is about renewing family bonds, unpacking
bequeathed treasures, enlarging our perspective
of Christ-following beyond modern fads, and finding clues to where the water of life is flowing these
days. It is about rediscovering the heroes of our
faith, getting to know them, and learning what they
can teach us. Surely this is why some branches of
the family of God set aside specific days to remem-

ber the lives of certain women and men who have lived passionately for Christ and his kingdom.

In this regard I give thankful testimony. During the early years of my Christ-following pilgrimage, there was minimal connection with the great minds and hearts from the past. I had little feeling for those who had borne bold witness for Christ after the New Testament era. My faith heroes were, without exception, contemporary. Gratefully, while preparing for the pastoral ministry, my attention was directed toward those wells from which life-giving water had once flowed. Soaking myself in these long-ago streams I found my passion for God refreshed and deepened.

The first stream to which I was drawn flowed through the Egyptian deserts. During the fourth and fifth centuries numerous Christ-followers, in their quest for a transforming experience of God, abandoned their ancient cities for the desert solitude. Around them desert communities began forming. Such was their contagious witness that thousands of seekers flocked to these desert fathers and mothers, as they were called, for counsel and direction. Reflecting on their lives and sayings immeasurably enriched my understanding of the Christ-focused life. While I knew that the desert option could never be considered literally normative for discipleship, it became clear that without "desert moments" of solitude and silence there would always be in my pilgrimage a certain superficiality and lack of depth. Encouraged by their example I began exploring for myself the experience of silent retreat, something that was quite foreign to my own faith tradition.

Where does one begin connecting with this "great cloud of witnesses"? I would respond simply. Every Christ-follower stands in one or another faith tradition—catholic, liturgical, evangelical, reformed, pentecostal. Discover where, when, and how in your own particular tradition the water of life initially flowed. Befriend those God-drenched women and men through whom genuine spiritual power once streamed. Identify the passions and practices that shaped their inner and outer lives. Discern those emphases, obscured perhaps by our modern prejudices and obsessions, that need to be freshly discovered for an authentic discipleship today. Finally, experiment in small ways with those treasures that you discover.

Participating in Your Local Congregation

God's gift of community is grounded within the relationship network of the local congregation. Community remains an abstract ideal unless it finds expression in real relationships. Singing "We are one in the Spirit" without embarking on the adventure of knowing and being known makes little sense. Christian community—fellowship—involves real-life people relating through the Holy One who enfolds our individual lives and provides our common meeting point.

Consider briefly the rich content of the familiar biblical word *fellowship*. Its strong meanings have been weakened almost beyond recognition. Mention the word to friends and colleagues and they will associate it with church committees, meetings, teas, and meals all held of course in the fellowship hall! Such events are not to be undermined but they do not demonstrate the rich realities to which the word points. *Koinonia,* the Greek equivalent for fellowship, refers to life-sharing with God and each other at the deepest levels. Using the human body as a model for relationships within the church, Paul captures vividly the potential richness of this life-sharing: "If one member suffers, all suffer together with it; if one part is honored, all rejoice together with it" (1 Cor. 12:26).

Participation within the general activities of the local congregation does not automatically bring about this kind of life-sharing. Church membership can often be nominal. Recently this was underlined afresh for me. Over an after-service cup of coffee I was chatting with a longtime member of our congregation. For over ten years this person has worshiped regularly, worked on committees, served at church functions. Yet he described his church experience in these words: "I feel a stranger at church. I don't feel I belong."

Some form of small-group involvement within the wider congregation seems crucial if genuine life-sharing is to occur. Such practice has solid biblical support. Describing the life of the early Christian community, Dr. Luke specifically observes that they assembled both in temple *and* home (Acts 2:46). These home gatherings suggest small companies of Christ-followers banding together for mutual encouragement, care, and celebration. In his spiritual direction to the Hebrews the author raises the question of ongoing conversion and recommends the way ahead in two sentences: "And let us consider how we may spur one another on toward love and good deeds. Let us not give up meeting together, as some are in the habit of doing, but let us encourage one another" (Heb. 10:24–25 NIV).

Establishing small groups requires caution. Not all facilitate healthy life-sharing. Some inhibit fellowship through authoritarian leadership, legalistic attitudes, and conformist pressures. Consequently these groups fail to create a safe, spacious, and sacred space for self-disclosure and honest conversation. Group life must be thoughtfully structured if it is going to realize its life-sharing purposes.

One model that evidences tremendous potential for growth in community is the gospel-sharing group.[4] Consisting of between three and eight people a gospel-sharing group nurtures relationship with the everliving Christ and a particular segment of his family. Not dependent on sophisticated leadership skills, advanced biblical knowledge, or gimmicky spiritual gadgetry, it enables everyday Christ-followers to accompany and support one another along the way. Through the exercise of personal sharing, believers use the Scriptures for the purpose of building up their faith within the experience of community. In the words of Scripture they seek to hear the Word, receive Christ into their lives, and discern what it means to follow him in the nitty-gritty of their daily lives. Different from the traditional Bible study/discussion group, the gospel-sharing group is uncomplicated in structure and method and can be plainly described, simply understood, and easily implemented.

Visit with me a neighborhood gospel-sharing group. When everyone has been welcomed, the group coordinator invites a spontaneous affirmation of Christ's presence among his people. "Will one or two please thank our Lord Jesus for being with us?" The gospel passage is introduced and group members, especially those with differing versions of the text, are asked to read it aloud, leisurely and prayerfully. In the third step, participants are encouraged to select a gospel word or phrase that strikes them personally, read it aloud slowly three times, and then listen attentively as others speak. In between individual contributions short periods of silence are observed to allow the words and phrases to reecho in the hearts of those present. After everyone has spoken the coordinator announces a clearly defined period of silence: "Let us now be silent together for five minutes as we allow God to speak to us." Following this communal silence, opportunity is given for each person to share, *without* comment from the group, what they have heard in their hearts and how they intend living their gospel word or phrase during the coming week. During this time there is also a report back regarding the past week's joys and struggles of living the gospel. Finally the group closes with shared prayer and the Lord's Prayer.

Recently I asked a professional woman, married with three young children, seriously desiring a God-yielded life, what weekly participation in a gospel-sharing group over a period of almost two years had meant to her. Her carefully phrased, written-out response personalizes the faith-building, life-transforming possibilities made available when we intentionally follow Christ together.

"My gospel-sharing group has helped me develop a firsthand relationship with God. It has initiated me into the value of actively listening to God and to my neighbor. I find myself more open to the struggles of others than ever before. I am learning to view my daily life through the eyes of Christ. In my efforts to follow him I feel less isolated. I know that others are bearing me up in their thoughts and prayers."

Building Faithful Friendships

Remember how Jesus, after inviting his disciples into intimate friendship with himself, commissions them in pairs (Luke 10:1). Faithful friendship lies at the very heart of the gospel. To use a delightful Quaker phrase, those early students of Jesus were "a society of friends." Christ-following, we learn from them, happens together, two by two. There are no solo journeys along the conversion road. While we are most certainly responsible for our own growth in discipleship, we do not mature into the people God wants us to be without the gifts that real friendship provides. One-to-one support, encouragement, and care are absolutely essential if our faith is to be kept strong and grow-

ing. The ancient author of Ecclesiasticus in the
Apocrypha was well aware of this. He writes,
"Faithful friends are a sturdy shelter: whoever
finds one has found a treasure. Faithful friends are
beyond price; no amount can balance their worth.
Faithful friends are life-saving medicine, and those
who fear the Lord will find them" (6:14–16).

But do we seek to find them? In the competitive, frantic, fast-lane scurry of everyday life, we
seldom carve out time and space for life-sharing
friendship. Last year this again became clear to
me when, together with a longtime psychologist
friend, I cohosted a forty-eight-hour men's life-
revision event. An afternoon was set aside for an
exploration of friendship. Before sharing experiences with a small group each participant examined his own friendship autobiography using a
few key questions. You may like to consider them:
Recall your most significant friendships. What
feelings do these memories evoke? Imagine what
it would be like to have greater depth, honesty,
and connectedness in your present friendships.
What are your blocks to friendship? Are you afraid
that people will think less of you if they were to
know the real you? How could you plan for a more
meaningful friendship without its becoming
problematic for spouse or partner? In a closing
plenary session after an afternoon of self-reflection

and small-group participation a middle-aged sales representative reflected wistfully: "Today I've realized that I have many acquaintances but no faithful friendships."

Perhaps you find yourself in a similar position and wonder how you could go about growing a faithful friendship. The first step is to choose someone. It is highly unlikely that you will drift into this kind of friendship. So begin to pray quite specifically about the matter. Ask God to lead you to someone with whom you can walk along the conversion road. Look around your circle of present acquaintances, those with whom you already interact at church or at work. Is there anyone who stands out as a possible companion on the way? During this time of praying and looking, keep the channels of communication open between you and those closest to you. It is important that they not feel threatened by your choice of a faithful friend. For this reason it may be wise to choose a friend of the same sex.

Once you have settled on a choice, the next step involves the risk of asking the person concerned whether they are open to the possibility of meeting regularly. This initial request needs to be clear, straightforward, and direct. I remember the first time I found myself on the receiving end of such a request from a colleague in ministry. "Trevor," he asked, "how would you feel about us getting together on a monthly basis over a cup of coffee to share with each other something of our lives and faith?" I felt comfortable with his request and we have been meeting now for several years. The friendship is deeply mutual, we refrain from trying to change each other, we share personal joys and struggles, and we promise to pray for each other. I do not seek to be his counselor or spiritual director, neither does he seek to fulfill these roles in my life. Our purpose is far more modest— we are seeking to be friends along the Way.

I hope that you have caught a glimpse of faithful friendship. Such friendship gradually unfolds as two people choose to spend time together, risk revealing their inner worlds, and allow themselves to be known for who they are. Becoming faithful friends is an adventure into personal vulnerability. It is not always easy. Often there are misunderstandings, disappointments, and unmet expectations. Like any real adventure the outcome is seldom a foregone conclusion. However, when we are with someone who accepts us as we are, listens attentively to what we share, and is committed to mutual interaction, courage is given for the first steps in this life-sharing enterprise.

Of all the God-given gifts provided to encourage us on the Christ-following way few equal the presence of faithful friends. Without faithful friendship we block the road to wholeness, fail to become all that God intends, and risk losing our Way. Without pilgrim companions our sense of the Christ-light in our lives can sometimes go out. Faithful friendship is God's disguised way of befriending us with his encouraging, life-enriching presence. "For where two or three are gathered in my name, I am there among them" (Matt. 18:20).

Belonging signposts the route toward becoming. An African proverb affirms scriptural wisdom when it says, "A person becomes a person through other people." There can be no I without you. Becoming truly human embraces the risks of life-sharing. Growing into fuller Christlikeness requires community. Little wonder, therefore, that on entering our yielded lives, the Christ of grace comes with arms around his brothers and sisters.

Following the Signpost Together

1. Write the word *church* on a sheet of newsprint. Brainstorm your immediate responses.
2. "We cannot be Christ-followers alone." Discuss your thoughts regarding this statement.
3. Discuss your sense of connection with the great spiritual heroes of the past.

4. How do you feel about the importance of "faithful friendship" for the spiritual journey?

5. End your time of group sharing with a time of gospel sharing. Select a passage from the Gospels and build a time of gospel sharing around it using the steps outlined in the chapter.

Becoming Holy, Becoming Ourselves

He was different. That is the only explanation I can offer for my school friend's faith-forming influence on my life. In his life I sensed qualities of depth, realness, and compassion that were missing from my own life and for which I longed. While we were walking home together from school one afternoon, these longings formed themselves into a searching question that was to launch me on my own spiritual journey: "How can I experience what makes your life different?"

Biblical writers would say that there was a holiness about my friend. Holiness is not mentioned much these days. The word tastes strange on our lips, sounds odd in casual conversations, and appears sidelined in much current Christian literature. This is surprising since in the Scriptures, God is the Holy One who wills holiness for each of us. Writing to scattered pilgrims, Peter quotes an ancient text that underlines this divine imperative: "You shall be holy, for I am holy" (1 Peter 1:16).

Recently I was part of a large group who were asked to brainstorm their spontaneous associations with the word *holiness.* Written feedback reflected the ambivalent feelings many have concerning the concept. On the lengthy list were words like guilt, perfection, faultless, a sense of failure, angelic, monks and nuns. In many people's minds holiness seems associated with an overly scrupulous, straitlaced, and ethereal lifestyle lacking any kind of attractiveness, vitality, or joy. Clearly there is need for a biblical perspective on the subject, a flesh-and-blood vision of what holiness looks like and, most importantly, a practical understanding of how we can grow into holiness.

Biblical revelation suggests that the single most important word to describe God is *holy.* Attending a communion service recently, I was struck again by the strange beauty of the eucharistic chant: "Holy, holy, holy; God of power and might; heaven and earth are full of your glory." The Hebrew word for holy, *qadosh,* emphasizes that God is essentially different. Engagement with the living God immerses us in a boundless mystery. There is really no one else like God. Holiness testifies to this sense of difference. So in Hosea God declares: "For I am God and no mortal, the Holy One in your midst" (Hosea 11:9).

But what is this essential difference? Recall our earlier reflections on the picture of God given us in Scripture. Mystery is not the final word spoken about God. New Testament faith declares the utter Christlikeness of God. At the heart of the Holy Mystery there is an immense and outrageous love that gives us life, accepts us as we are, draws us forward into wholeness, and will never let us go. The fire of God's holiness is the fire of blazing love. God is set apart from us by self-giving love. Donald McCullough describes succinctly this essential difference: "God is holy because he loves and loves because he is holy. The Wholly Other is wholly for us."[1]

The Human Face of Holiness

Jesus, the holy servant, as Dr. Luke *twice* describes him, joins heaven and earth together, gives holiness a human face, and offers insight regarding its shape in our daily lives. Notice therefore the three deeply interwoven threads of holy living as the figure of Jesus emerges from the pages of the Gospels. *First, throughout his earthly life Jesus is his own person.* He is the same person inside and outside, never wears masks, and is always his real and true self. By his example he sets us free from any form of carbon copy holiness that would seek to diminish our individuality. Rather, to be holy in a Christlike way is in fact to become more truly ourselves. Holiness has little in common with pharisaic rule keeping, stuffy churchianity, or sterile ritual. But it has everything to do, if we take the example of Jesus seriously, with the glorious freedom of growing into our true selves and becoming the people that God wants us to be.

A delightful Hasidic tale reinforces this truth. When Rabbi Zusya arrived in heaven, as the legend goes, he was anxious about the degree of his holiness. He wondered whether God was going to reprimand him. He imagined God angrily cross-examining him about his way of life, "Tell me why did you not become like Moses or Solomon or David?" However, when God approached the rabbi the question was altogether different. "Tell me," asked God quietly, "why did you not become Rabbi Zusya?"

Second, notice the way in which Jesus the holy servant relates to others. He mingles easily with people from all social strata, enjoys socializing over a good meal at dinner parties, and constantly has time for little children. Outcasts feel relaxed and at ease in his company, while those who have messed up their lives seem to sense that they are unconditionally accepted. His relationships are consistently characterized by awareness, insight, and responsiveness: noticing a man hiding in a tree, seeing into the painful entanglements of a woman aching for intimacy, hearing the anguished cry of a blind beggar above the din of a noisy crowd. Gospel holiness touches others with compassion and care. To become holy the Christlike way is to become increasingly less self-centered and more concerned about the needs around us. When we are more interested in giving than in receiving, our lives begin to transmit the holiness of Christ.

Notice finally that at the center of Jesus' life there is a devoted closeness with the Holy One whom he experiences directly as Abba and whose kingdom is his dearest passion. This intimate friendship between Jesus and his Father is the holy hub of his entire life. The gospel records indicate that Jesus was concerned with only one thing: to do the will of the Father. Listen again to some of his recorded words. "Did you not know that I must be in my Father's house?" (Luke 2:49); "Very truly, I tell you, the Son can do nothing on his own, but only what he sees the Father doing; for whatever the Father does, the Son does likewise" (John 5:19); "The word that you hear is not mine, but is from the Father who sent me" (John 14:24); "Father, into your hands I commend my spirit" (Luke 23:46). Unless we nurture our intimacy with the Holy One, holiness remains out of reach. Holy men and women are those for whom God comes first.

Transformed by His Spirit

How do we come to share in the holiness of Christ? There are two sides to the answer of this important question. On the one side we must affirm that in this holy-making process it is Christ by his Spirit who transforms us. Holiness is not a do-it-yourself job. As we turn toward Christ and entrust ourselves to him, he comes to live within us in the power of his Spirit. Remaining open and yielded to this Spirit of transformation is absolutely crucial for the serious Christ-follower. Through his loving power we are gradually transformed into our true selves, fashioned into instruments of his love, and nourished in our relationship with the Holy One. Holiness is an inside work of the Spirit, a gracious gift to those who live with open hands. Paul makes this clear when he writes these words, "And all of us, with unveiled faces, seeing the glory of the Lord as though reflected in a mirror, are being transformed into the same image from one degree of glory to another; for this comes from the Lord, the Spirit" (2 Cor. 3:18).

Yet the moment we grasp this liberating insight we must not fall into the tragic error of saying that there is nothing we can do. Holiness does not just happen. Hence the other side of our answer must affirm our part in the holy-making process. Faith without action is dead. The spiritual journey demands a great deal of human effort. Personal transformation requires our determined and planned cooperation. We have to work at becoming all that we are meant to be. Compassion is not for the lazy and passive. Growing in our relationship with the Holy One occurs only when we take appropriate measures for this to happen. The author of Hebrews stresses the human side of our answer when he encourages his readers to "make every effort . . . to be holy" (Heb. 12:14 NIV).

But what are we to do? God has graciously given to us, in the life of Jesus, activities through which we can open our hearts more widely to the Spirit's transforming presence. Often described as "disciplines for the spiritual life," these activities enable us to place our lives more consciously before God so that we can be changed. Many helpful books describing these practices are available for the serious seeker.[2] I want to highlight two such activities, many times neglected and overlooked, that are crucial for an authentic expression of Christlike holiness: space alone in God's presence and exposure to the sufferings of others.

Alone in God's Presence

Carving out space in our activity-filled lives to be alone with God is a vital ingredient of the

Christ-following life. In spite of enormous pressures and ministry demands, the story of Jesus' life is punctuated with such spaces: retreating for forty days into desert silence, spending a night alone before selecting his twelve companions, withdrawing before sunrise to a solitary place following an exhausting day's ministry, seeking the solitude of the Gethsemane garden before the Calvary victory. These moments of silence and solitude were the secret of his life. In them Jesus was able to nurture his intimate communion with Abba, replenish his resources for compassionate ministry, wrestle with that dark tempting voice intent on enticing him into illusion, and renew his body in restful relaxation. If Jesus needed these spaces, surely our need is even greater.

Choosing to step away from human interaction—withdrawing attention from the outer world and becoming quieter, trusting that God is both graciously present and tremendously active—has life-transforming benefits. Time is given for the seeking of God's mind on decisions, issues, and conflicts that must be faced. Other spiritual disciplines—study, reflective reading and meditation, prayer, journaling, Sabbath-resting, dream interpretation—can only be faithfully practiced if this one is firmly set in place. Solitude and the silence inside it enables an exploration of our shadow selves, which, as we have already seen, is a pre-requisite for traveling along the conversion road of the kingdom. We are put in touch with all kinds of previously unrecognized thoughts and feel-ings—jealousy, envy, lust, revenge, anger lurking in our subterranean depths—that God wants us to own. Then God wants to totally transform us as his Holy Spirit occupies our lives.

I am a beginner in these matters of silence and solitude. Carving out empty spaces does not come easily for me. Recently I allowed myself to get snarled up in a whirlwind of compulsive busy-ness. For almost two weeks I neglected my daily discipline of sitting quietly with Scripture and journal. From early until late I juggled commit-ments, dashed here and there responding to crises, and raced to meet deadlines. A simple dream stopped me in my tracks: I was driving my Datsun when suddenly I had a blow-out, which sent my car careening dangerously across the road. Thankfully, as the wisdom of the Song of Songs reminds us, even as we sleep the heart keeps watch—often through these visions given in the night. The next day I put the brakes on, halted my busyness, sat myself down in an empty nearby chapel, and read the inner gauges. In my journal I scribbled out my prayer: "Lord, thank you for that warning dream. It's good to be sitting silently here again. I confess that I have been living hurriedly and distractedly. I feel out of touch with my own depths and with your indwelling presence. I seem to be running around continuously, trying to meet everyone else's demands but not living my own life. I see now as I sit here that I am sometimes more interested in establishing my importance than in serving you. I am sorry, Lord, and want to make a fresh beginning. Help me, Lord, to discern what drives me into hurry. And as I seek to carve out in my life those empty spaces that I need, please give me your wisdom."

Does my experience echo in any way your own? We live fast, frenetic, and filled lives, which inwardly strangle the recreating presence of the Spirit. We find it difficult to stop. Yet it is something we must learn to do. I still remember the first bit of advice that I received when I began learning to drive. "The first thing you need to know," said my driving instructor, "is how to stop." The same principle applies to our journey along the Way with Christ. Donald Nicholl writes, "Unless we can stop the rush and noise of daily traffic in our lives we do not have the slightest chance of hearing the call to holiness."[3] Unfortunately many of us keep delaying that time when we can bring our lives to a halt and stop and listen to what's going on inside of them.

Do not delay! Take time to stop now. A story from the Egyptian deserts drives this point home in a rather delightful way. One day a harassed and busy executive was on his way to his office when he spotted a bedouin from the desert sitting and resting under a city-park tree. The executive stopped and asked the bedouin, "What are you doing here?"

"Well, as you can see," answered the bedouin, "I've decided to stop for a while."

"You know that you could be earning money if you were working," said the executive.

"What would I do with it?"

"If you earned some money you could open an office."

"And then?"

"Then you could earn more money and build a factory."

"And then?"

"Then you could have your own villa at some fancy resort."

"Good, and then?"

"Then you would still have some money to put in the bank."

"Yes, and then?"

"Well, then you could stop, sit down, and rest."

"But that's what I'm doing at the moment."[4]

Stop for a moment and consider some questions that I find immeasurably helpful in my endeavors toward a less breathless, more leisurely, evenly paced way of life. When do I catch myself hurrying? Why am I so often living in a hurry mode? What patterns of greed or avoidance are revealed in my hurriedness? How can I rearrange my daily activities in order to carve out some "stopping moments" for myself? Wrestling with these questions may lead into a few modest commitments: taking time on waking to jot down the night's dream, pausing at the beginning of each new activity and reminding oneself of God's immediate presence, withdrawing before work or at lunch break for fifteen minutes of silence and prayer, replaying before falling asleep the day's encounters and events, and noticing where God has been present in grace and blessing. For those who struggle to be quiet on their own, joining a gospel-sharing group with its opportunities for silent reflection on Scripture could prove helpful. Embarking on steps like these puts our feet on that pathway described by Isaiah as the "Way of Holiness" (Isa. 35:8 NIV).

One rather radical way of stopping the rush and noise of daily traffic in our lives is to plan a desert day. This would involve planning to spend an entire day in silence and solitude. Obviously this requires careful consultation with loved ones, wise arrangements for their welfare, and thoughtful plans that ensure legitimate responsibilities are well cared for. Then a suitable place to which one can retreat must be located. This could be a nearby retreat center, the grounds and facilities of one's local church, or the quiet backyard of a friend's home. Structure the day itself carefully with time set aside for rest and reflection, exercise, and prayer. Perhaps the day could begin with the leisurely reading of a portion of Scripture that you want to keep resounding in your depths throughout the day—a psalm, a gospel story, a portion of a letter. Write down in a notebook insights that come from your engagement with the Scriptures and also the thoughts that pop into your mind during the silence of the day. Writing these things down tends to bring clarity and direction in our thinking. Experiencing the benefits of a desert day encourages our commitment to build "stopping moments" into our everyday lives.

Exposure to the Sufferings of Others

Any spiritual journey that removes the Christ-follower from human suffering is counterfeit and delusive. It betrays God's passionate love for every person, denies our connectedness in the human family, and results in what has been described as "a false inwardness."[5] We become the person God intends, not inside a private religious zone, but within God's broken and wounded world. Becoming holy opens eyes blind to Christ's presence in suffering people, increases awareness of our neighbor's pain, and draws the Christ-follower into the human struggles of the day. John Wesley, hugely instrumental in the eighteenth century evangelical awakening, would constantly insist, "there is no holiness but social holiness."

Jesus, the holy servant, makes this clear. We have observed his practice of frequently punctuating his ministry life with empty spaces. These moments were never selfish or escapist. Intimacy nurtured with Abba in silence and solitude streamed outward in compassionate responsiveness. Two gospel sentences placed in close proximity in Mark's opening chapter portray powerfully the inward-outward journey dynamic so characteristic of Jesus' life. The first reads matter of factly: "Very early in the morning, while it was still dark, Jesus got up, left the house and went off to a solitary place" (v. 35 NIV). Six verses later we read: "Filled with compassion, Jesus reached out his hand and touched the [leper]" (v. 41 NIV).

Compassion is evidence of the holy life. The Christ-like person formed gradually by the Spirit will be characterized by an ever growing responsiveness and sensitivity to the pain of others.

Compassion extends beyond fleeting feelings of sympathy and pity. Compassion, in the way of Jesus, places our lives beside those in turmoil, seeks understanding of their anguish, and labors with them for the sake of their greater wholeness. Without disciplined effort it is doubtful whether we shall touch another in this way. God infuses our hearts with divine compassion as opportunities are made available.

Exposing our lives intentionally to the sufferings of others is one practical way of doing this. Jesus himself practiced this activity and, in his crucified-risen presence, promises to meet us wherever people are in need (Matt. 25:40). I learned the value of this spiritual discipline through a decade's involvement with The Pilgrimage of Pain and Hope. Throughout the traumatized '80s of our country's history these pilgrimages were an integral part of our congregational life. More than one hundred young, and not so young, adults participated. The event became an instrument of lasting personal transformation.

The Pilgrimage of Pain and Hope is an eight-day journey of two-fold encounter. First, it is an encounter with the pain of our shattered and fragmented society. Usually the pilgrims come from backgrounds that have shielded them from the harsh realities of the South African context.

Poverty, destitution, and homelessness tend to be abstractions in their experience, as they are in my own. Many of the pilgrims have never related their Christ-following to these social realities, nor have they had the experience of sharing life with and learning from those who know firsthand the pain of these social contexts.

Second, the Pilgrimage is an encounter with hope. Scattered throughout these deprived communities are those who resiliently refuse to become prisoners of hopelessness. Often unsung and anonymous, these people have suffered and struggled for a new South Africa. Encountering these signs of hope challenges the pilgrims to examine their own faith-responses within the present historical moment. They learn that the future is open-ended and that their lives can make a creative difference in a land torn apart by division and suffering.

Reflection on experience is a critical ingredient in the Pilgrimage process. Daily the pilgrims experience a wide range of emotions, circumstances, and people. Without reflection they run the risk of losing those insights that empower these experiences to transform us. Questions are given that facilitate the reflection process. What did we do today? What encounter made the deepest impression on me? What person left a lasting impression? What actions of hope and obedience did I see? What do I sense Christ saying to me through my day's experiences? At the beginning of each day when the group gathers for worship these reflections are shared. Here feelings are expressed and worked through, questions asked, issues clarified, and dreams for future actions of obedience articulated.

While we can plan into the Pilgrimage the elements of encounter and reflection, we cannot ensure the experience of transformation. Transformation into the likeness of Christ is a gift that happens in those generously open to the Holy One. When there is this openness among the pilgrims it is our testimony that the Spirit transforms hearts and lives. Many stories can be shared. A seventeen-year-old high school drop-out reports, "The Pilgrimage brought home to me the stark reality in which many live. No longer is suffering a list of cold statistics." A young teacher describes his experience in these words: "I saw what mattered in life. I began to feel in a new way what others go through. When I returned home I battled with the superficiality of my cultural surroundings." An intern doctor reflects, "I realized that it is not enough to be shocked or indignant at the circumstances of people who suffer. If I am to seriously follow Christ I must be prepared to give my life in sacrificial service."

Not everyone can go away on an eight-day pilgrimage. Nonetheless we can build into our lives
the discipline of planned encounter with those
who suffer in our midst. We begin to practice this
discipline by committing ourselves to spend some
time each week with someone who suffers deeply.
This person may be elderly and alone, terminally
ill, severely handicapped, desperately poor, or
stuck in dark depression. Rather than doing things
for the person, the emphasis of our time together
is on being there, actively listening, and seeking
understanding. As we give ourselves to this activity, believing that God will meet us, we receive
more fully into our lives the transforming power
of the Spirit.

I encourage you to set up for yourself a holy
experiment in this regard. Think of someone who
presently suffers and whom you are able to contact. Arrange to spend time with this person.
When you make personal contact, adopt the
stance of a pilgrim. You are with this person, not
to give her advice or to make things right, but to
learn from her what it is like to be in her situation.
Seek to listen rather than to speak. Remind yourself that the Holy One is present in the sufferings
of the sufferer. Do not underestimate what your
simple presence may mean. After the visit, take
time to reflect on it, write out your feelings and

thoughts, and ask God if there is anything you need to learn from the experience.

God's transformation of our lives is both painful and joyfully liberating. Exposure to the sufferings of others connects us with our own grief and fear. We are brought face-to-face with the immense forces of selfishness and prejudice that lurk inside us all. We discover the hardness of our own heart and its capacity for evildoing and destruction. And yet it is precisely in those parched and barren places that, if our hands remain open, God quietly goes about transforming our hearts. The implanted seed of divine compassion begins to flower. Nonsentimental and caring deeds are birthed. Courage is given to speak truth to those principalities and powers intent on destroying the lives of people. Our hearts begin yearning for a society where there is justice and compassion for all. That this can begin to happen in our lives is the testimony of our pilgrims.

The Longing to Be Different

Holiness arouses longing and sorrow. Encountering God-touched men and women who are different for the sake of Christ and his kingdom always disturbs. Their depth exposes our superficiality, their realness uncovers our falseness, their compassion reveals our self-centeredness.

In their presence we long to be different. These holy longings cry out for fulfillment. The good news is that the Spirit of God who dwells inside these longings wants very much to give us experiences of transformation and change. They are given to those who genuinely seek the Holy One in solitude and in the suffering of their neighbors. What is essential is that we begin the seeking.

Following the Signpost Together

1. Write the word *holiness* on a sheet of paper. Brainstorm your immediate responses to this word.
2. Discuss the flesh and blood vision of holiness that we see in the life of Jesus of Nazareth. In what ways does the holiness of Christ revise our traditional understanding of this word?
3. Share your experience of the Holy Spirit in your life.
4. In what ways do you avoid the experience of silence and solitude?
5. What have you learned from suffering people?

As a group you may want to make yourselves accountable with regard to some of the practical suggestions outlined in the chapter.

Loving Those Closest to Us

C ompassionate caring is the acid test of the authentic Christ-following life. Practices of spiritual disciplines that do not result in others, especially those closest to us, feeling more valued and loved are hollow and empty. Genuine growth in relationship with the Holy One evidences itself primarily in an ever-deepening capacity to care for others. When this does not happen we have failed the acid test.

I once visited the home of a man with a devout reputation. Vocal in expressing his faith, regular in his church commitments, and enthusiastic about evangelism, he had become a key figure in his local congregation. During our visit the phone rang. It was his pastor requesting his immediate presence. An urgent matter had arisen requiring prompt attention. As he left the house I was left alone with his wife, a rather tired looking woman in her early fifties. One exchange in our brief conversation remains fresh in my memory.

"Your husband is certainly a deeply committed man," I casually remarked as we heard her husband's car speeding down the street. For a few moments she was quiet. I thought I sensed a hidden and smoldering resentment. Her sharp response confirmed my intuition.

"Yes, I guess you can say that. But then you don't have to live with him on a daily basis."

We do well not to judge the man. Have there not been numerous occasions in our own personal lives when those closest to us have felt neglected, unloved, and taken for granted? I recall one painful moment in my own marriage. I had just assumed responsibility for my first congregation. Obviously keen to succeed I worked long, hard hours. Externally, things were going well. Attendance was increasing, finances had improved, and a new sanctuary was on the drawing board. Within my marriage relationship, however, I was not doing well. Often away from home I was denying the person closest to me the attention, time, and energy necessary for real communication and caring. Coming home late one night I found a note at my bedside table. It read simply: "Trevor I love you and want to be married to you. Sometimes I worry though that one day I may not be worried if you don't come home. I miss you and want to reconnect." I had failed the acid test.

Challenged to Love

Learning to love particular individuals is an indispensable component of the Christ-following vocation. God, as we have already noted, is extravagantly, sacrificially, and unconditionally loving. Jesus, God come in the flesh, lived this love and taught what he lived. The language of the kingdom is the language of self-giving love. Participation in this kingdom demands one central commitment. It requires sharing with others the same kind of compassion, mercy, and caring that we have received from God. This is the essential distinguishing characteristic, the acid test, as I've called it, of being a follower of Jesus. Ponder again those startling words spoken by Jesus, "A new commandment I give you: Love one another. As I have loved you, so you must love one another. All men will know that you are my disciples if you love one another" (John 13:34–35 NIV).

This great commandment is given us for our wholeness, the well-being of our relationships, and the healing of our societies. Shaping our lives into instruments of God's love breaks the tyranny of ingrained self-centeredness and narcissism. We step out of our cramped and suffocating worlds into the spacious milieu of the kingdom. We begin blossoming into the mature people God wants us to be. Our lives come alive with renewed responsiveness and fresh meaning. We discover how loving others releases within them immense possibilities for growth and change. And we realize that only the power of God's love, manifest in the lives of ordinary people, can heal our broken world. Mmutlanyane Mogoba describes love as "the Great Transformer of the Global Village." There is no higher priority for the Christ-follower than learning to love.

Elton Trueblood is a widely read Quaker author whose writings have influenced the lives of countless women and men. Now in the ninth decade of his life he continues to encourage others through the writing of a quarterly newsletter. In his newsletter dated June 1994 he describes a banquet dinner given in his honor where he told the story of his own life, calling it "A Life of Search." Profoundly moved by the spirit of loving commitment that joined together the three hundred people who had gathered for this occasion, Elton Trueblood was prompted to write about the crucial priority of becoming a loving person. After quoting the many New Testament texts that support this central emphasis on love, he writes these moving words:

> At the age of 93 I am well aware that I do not have many years to live. Consequently, I try very hard to live my remaining years in such a manner that I make a real difference in as many lives as possible. How do I want to be remembered? Not primarily as a Christian scholar, but rather as a loving person. This can be the goal of every individual. If I can be remembered as a truly loving person I shall be satisfied. Now I hope

that this Quarterly Letter may help others to realize what comes first in the life of a Christian. The great idea is that a life of love is really open to all. Every individual who reads this letter can try to be more loving.[1]

What does it mean, as the Ephesians author writes, to "live a life of love, as Christ loved us" (Eph. 5:2 NIV)? Wrestling with this question moves one from the abstract to the concrete, from the universal to the particular, from theory to practice. I have struggled with this question for almost twenty years. Conscious that my greatest failures have been those in loving, it is with a certain reserve that I offer the following three suggestions. Representing my own development they arise from an ongoing engagement with the gospel story, insights gleaned from mentors along the way, and reflection on personal experiences of being loved and learning to love. In this chapter I focus particularly on loving those closest to us—spouse, child, parent, brother, sister, partner, faithful friend. Something is radically wrong if we talk about caring within the wider community and neglect those in our intimate circle.

Begin with Confession

Confessing our inability to love the Jesus way connects us to God's resources and strengthens us on the loving way. Despite humankind's massive advances in knowledge and technology, there is one area where we remain immature and ignorant: *We do not know how to love.* Personal experience confirms biblical insight. Inside us all, there are powerful, ingrained forces that block the flow of self-giving love, sabotage efforts at fostering intimacy, and repeatedly alienate us from those with whom we live. We want to love yet constantly fail. It would appear, as Paul confesses in the seventh chapter of his letter to the Romans, that there rages within the human heart a fierce tug-of-war to claim or to forfeit the loving destinies God intends for every one of us (Rom. 7:13–25).

This struggle is humorously and pointedly illustrated in a delightful *Peanuts* cartoon: Lucy has drawn a large picture of a heart on a wooden fence and is describing it to Linus. One side is filled with hate and the other side is filled with love. She explains excitedly, "There are the two forces which are constantly at war with each other." Linus listens attentively to this and then with his tongue out, his hair disarranged, and his hands pressed against his heart, he exclaims, "I think I know just what you mean . . . I can feel them fighting myself."

The cartoon portrays the good and bad news about our lives. There is the side that genuinely seeks to care and give itself away in self-forgetful compassion. This is our truest nature, the image of God imprinted on our souls, the person God wants us to be. There is also that side with its infinite capacity for self-centeredness, which curves us inward on ourselves, imprisons us in egoism, and hobbles our attempts at loving. In an earlier chapter we called this our sin-condition. When estranged from the source of love it is the latter side that consistently triumphs. The more it wins the stronger it grows. Evil finds a firmer foothold in our lives. Damage is inflicted on those around us and on ourselves. Our immense potential for living and loving God's way is wasted. Without help from beyond ourselves we miss the mark that God has set for our lives.

Only those, I would dare suggest, who acknowledge their impoverishment when it comes to loving, and come repeatedly into the presence of the Holy One with open hands learn to care in the spirit of Jesus. This is not easy. Admitting failures and weaknesses in loving can be humiliating. Letting go of virtuous illusions about ourselves is tough. Relinquishing rationalizations and excuses leaves us vulnerable. Taking back blame heaped on others for not meeting our needs confronts us with the challenge of sacrificial caring. However, we are encouraged in these processes by the knowledge that God in Christ is utterly for us, accepts us in our lovelessness, and offers us moment by moment his empowering companionship.

A childlike exercise enables me to appropriate the resourcing benefits of confession. I learned this exercise from Morton Kelsey, Episcopalian priest and prolific author, who has written helpfully about the challenges of caring.[2] Involving our imagination, it is based on a familiar passage of the New Testament, written by John in the last book of the Bible and sent as a message to some lukewarm disciples as a message from the risen Jesus himself: "Listen! I am standing at the door knocking; if you hear my voice and open the door, I will come in to you and eat with you, and you with me" (Rev. 3:20). After reading through the way I have adapted this exercise for my own use, you may want to take a few minutes and practice it yourself where you are.

I imagine myself to be sitting alone in my own soul-room. Its darkness and untidiness represent my failure in reaching out compassionately and lovingly to those around me. As I look around at the clothes lying on the floor, the unmade bed, the cluttered washbasin, there is a dark voice that accuses me, "Trevor, you really are no good at Christ-following. Look at the way you disappoint those closest to you, fail to love them, and let them down. Forget about following Christ and trying to live his way of love. It will never work for you." I hear that voice often in my moments of failure and dis-obedience. Whenever I hear it I am learning to respond firmly, "Keep quiet. You are a lying, deceiv-ing voice, and I will not allow you to define my life."

As this dark voice fades I hear another sound— a gentle persistent knocking at the door of my soul-room. When I ask the guest to enter he answers that he cannot, for the door is locked and the latch is inside. I realize that this guest is not a burglar who wants to intrude. He awaits my invitation to enter my life. Opening the door I am greeted by the risen Lord. He still bears the scars of crucifixion, and his continuing love for me is clear. The light of his pres-ence shines into the darkness of my room.

"Dear Lord," I say to him, "my soul-room is a mess, but please come in." He enters, puts his arm around my shoulders, and leads me to a table amid the mess, where we sit down. With quiet authority my guest becomes the host. In Emmaus-like fashion bread is broken, wine is poured, and we commune together. An inner assurance that I am loved, forgiven, and accepted rises in my heart. I start sharing specifically about the many ways in which I withhold myself from those I love, the symptoms of my self-centeredness, my uncaring thoughts and attitudes. After listening attentively he tells me not to give up. He will give me his transforming Spirit and will empower me anew for the tasks of loving.

As I conclude the exercise with a prayer of thankfulness I usually feel renewed in faith, hope, and love. I am ready to begin again. There are times, though, when I feel stuck in my struggles to become a loving person. Sharing these struggles with a faithful friend who will listen and pray with me helps tremendously. James may have had this kind of sharing in mind when he taught those belonging to the early church to "confess your sins to each other" (James 5:16 NIV). Our failure to become open, vulnerable, caring people could well be related to our resistance toward doing this. Confession—whether it happens in the inner sanctuary of our soul or in the presence of another—opens clogged channels between God and us, allows for the inpouring of his love, and resources us anew for the work of love.

Listen Carefully

The Scriptures are clear: The God who loves is the God who listens. The biblical God, whose face we have seen in Jesus, hears the cry of the oppressed, listens to the distress of the psalmist, and is attentive even to those groans we cannot put into words. Jesus lived in the constant awareness of this listening presence. "Father," he once prayed, "I thank you that you have heard me. I knew that you always hear me" (John 11:41–42 NIV). God joins love and listening inseparably together and what God has joined together let no person put asunder.

Listening is one of the most precious gifts that we can give to someone we love. Stop for a moment and recall your own feelings when you last felt truly listened to. When this experience is ours we feel valued for who we are, recognized as a unique human being, and affirmed as a God-created person. Listening says to the other person, *I care for you. I respect your uniqueness. How you feel and what you say matters to me. And in order to make this clear, I'm willing to set aside my own concerns, give you space to share yourself, and offer you my focused attention. I want to try to understand the inexhaustible mystery of your inner world.*

Consciously making the effort to listen well involves three basic ground rules: respectful silence, total attention, and appropriate response.[3] Unless we bridle our tongue, restrain ourselves from interrupting, and become quiet inside, it is impossible even to begin listening. Unless we concentrate intently on what someone is saying—the feelings that accompany the words and the silences in between them—genuine listening seldom occurs. Unless we indicate some understanding of what is being said and felt in our verbal response, it is improbable that the person will feel listened to. This kind of real listening makes empathy possible.

Empathetic listening is difficult, requires persistent effort, and takes time to learn. Few people are able to listen effectively without practical guidance and experiential training. Strangely enough the local congregation is often the last place where classes in listening are provided. We talk more about the "gift of tongues" and little about the "gift of ears"! The observation of Dietrich Bonhoeffer, German pastor and martyr, made over fifty years ago continues to be strikingly relevant: "Many people are looking for an ear that will listen. They do not find it among Christians, because Christians are talking when they should be listening."[4]

If I am to give this kind of quality listening to those closest to me, we will need uninterrupted time together. Making an appointment with loved ones is one practical way of ensuring this happens. On my weekly day off, my wife and I have an appointment for breakfast. Few practices have enriched our relationship more than this simple arrangement. It gives us a leisurely opportunity to share and to listen. I'm discovering that appointments with my children create the space for similar listening and sharing. When I commend this practice to other couples in counsel-

ing sessions, I am frequently surprised how few
have thought of making such an appointment.

Rooted in Action

"My children," teaches John, beloved disciple
and wise spiritual guide, "our love should not be
just words and talk; it must be true love, which
shows itself in action" (1 John 3:18 TEV). Jesus
enfleshed these words. His love was a love-in-
action. He touched lepers, shared meals with
outsiders, hugged children, fed hungry people,
washed dirty feet, and ultimately laid his life
down on a cross for us all. Love meant far more
for Jesus than a fleeting feeling, a sentimental
thought, a wishful emotion. Love implied a priority decision and commitment to act in a loving way that would leave others feeling valued
and important.

Love in action is chiefly a matter of the will. Jesus
invites decision and commitment when he commands us to love as he loved. This commandment
does not address our feelings and emotions. Not
that these are unimportant. There are times when
we do feel warm and affectionate and these feelings need to be expressed. However, loving actions
are not dependent on good feelings. There are
many moments when the Christ-follower inwardly

decides: No matter how I may be feeling, with God's help, I commit myself to act in a loving way.

Earlier this month I celebrated my birthday. The day before had been an exceptionally busy one for my wife—entertaining the wider family for lunch, shopping in the mall, overseeing the children while I fulfilled some outside ministry obligations. By the end of the day she was exhausted. I knew that she felt like getting into bed and falling asleep. In spite of her weariness, I noticed her going to the living room with scissors, card, glue, and old magazines. Early the next morning I was awakened with a hug and the gift of a homemade card. Debbie had extended herself and, in spite of feeling weary and tired, acted in a loving way. I felt appreciated, valued, and loved.

I deliberately choose a very ordinary episode from our family life together to illustrate my point. The ways in which we commit ourselves to be channels of God's love are usually down to earth. Characterized by thoughtfulness, creativity, and kindness, they are within the reach of us all: cooking a favorite meal, buying a surprise gift, writing an overdue letter, remembering an anniversary, giving space for a loved one to be alone, and yes, creating a homemade birthday card! Simple actions like these are sacramental. They connect us with God's loving presence and give us a taste of the heavenly banquet. Apostle John describes the experience in a single sentence: "Those who abide in love abide in God and God abides in them" (1 John 4:16).

Take a few moments to engage in a holy experiment designed to unite our praying and loving. It could well open your life and relationship to the creative power of God's kingdom. I find it helpful to repeat this experiment at regular intervals. Begin by asking God for the discernment that the Spirit gives. List the names of those with whom you share most closely your daily life. According to your best knowledge of each person think about his or her individual hopes and needs. Write down next to each person's name what practical expression of caring would most contribute to his or her greater wholeness. Without fuss go about putting these written intentions into practice. Allow these actions to become channels of that extravagant love and gracious acceptance that we have been given by God. Reflect on the results of the experiment, asking God to guide you as you continue seeking to be an instrument of his love in your close relationships.

Caring for those closest to us signposts us toward genuine growth in God. Through confession, empathetic listening, and caring actions we embark on the loving way. Stepping into this world of compassion we step into the world of the self-giving God. Miracles of the Spirit begin to occur. Our lives and relationships are gifted with healing and newness. Hearts of stone become hearts of flesh. We pass the acid test.

Following the Signpost Together

1. What do you think about the statement, "There is no higher priority for the Christ-follower than learning to love"?

2. Share one struggle you have in loving those closest to you.

3. What blocks you from listening actively to those with whom you relate most deeply?

4. "Loving actions are not dependent on good feelings." How do you respond?

5. End your time by sharing together as a group in the imaginative meditation outlined in the chapter. (It may be helpful if someone in the group has prepared this meditation beforehand and then leads the rest of the group through it.)

Discovering God's Call for Our Lives

ecently I watched a television documentary portraying the remarkable life and ministry of Mother Teresa among the suffering poor of Calcutta. At one stage there is a poignant exchange between her and the commentator. He asks whether she does not find her work futile and hopeless given the immensity of the task facing her and the sisters. In her typically humble fashion she replies, "I was not called to be successful but faithful. Each one of us has something beautiful to do for God."

You are not alone if you struggle to believe this for yourself. Often we feel our smallness, are filled with self-doubt, and have little sense of ourselves as instruments of God's kingdom in his suffering world. So when someone like Mother Teresa suggests that God has something special for each of us to accomplish we are only half-convinced. Yet her words signpost the inescapable challenge facing every Christ-follower: to discern the task God wants him or her to fulfill.

Call is the biblical word that describes this challenge. It is a central scriptural theme that threads its way through the actions of all the key figures in its pages. Abraham was called, as was Moses, as was Jeremiah, as was Mary, as were the early disciples. We are not excluded. Writing to the enthusiastic Corinthian congregation Paul makes clear that every Christ-follower is a called person: "Let each of you lead the life that the Lord has assigned, to which God has called you" (1 Cor. 7:17).

After opening our lives to the crucified-risen Lord and his family we are invited into a threefold vocation: Become the person God wants us to be, care for those closest to us as Christ has loved us, *and* participate in God's kingdom-dream for a healed and healing society. Earlier chapters sought to probe the first two components of this Christ-following adventure. Exploring the third involves clarifying the biblical features of personal calling, unraveling its relationship with our daily job, and finally offering some practical suggestions for discerning and following this call in our individual lives.

Personal Calling in the Bible

God has a kingdom assignment in mind for you and me. This good work, which has our unique name written across it, is our personal calling. An ancient Christian tradition celebrates this truth when it states that God sends every person into the world with a special message to deliver, with a special song to sing for others, with a special act of love to bestow. No one else can speak my message, or sing my song, or offer my act of love. These are entrusted only to me.[1] Paul puts forward the biblical basis for the tradition in a single sentence: "For we are what he has made us, created in Christ Jesus for good works, which God prepared beforehand to be our way of life" (Eph. 2:10).

Do you not intuitively sense this truth stirring in your own depths? Underneath persistent feelings of emptiness and unfulfillment there often lies hidden the unexplored treasure that is one's personal calling. Just this past week a regular participant in the weekly activities of our congregation sought an interview to share the discontent of her soul. One sentence, spoken tentatively and almost shyly, stayed with me long after she had left my study: "I feel that God has something special for me to do but I don't seem able to put my finger on what it is."

Before unpacking four biblical features that describe God's personal calling in our lives, I must note one important exception to what has so far been written. Those in deep depression and those who are mentally ill are often unable to wrestle with the challenges of personal calling. Sometimes it is even difficult for them to experience any kind of significant relatedness with the Holy One. One of the most important tasks in our local congregation is to provide caring for those who find themselves mentally and emotionally unable to engage their calling. Often in our excitement about what God is calling us to do, we very easily neglect or overlook those around us who simply don't have the available resources to deal with these kinds of faith issues. Indeed there may well be those in the local congregation for whom caring for the depressed and mentally ill is their primary call.

Discovering our personal calling nourishes our lives and those of others. This biblical feature of personal calling finds its origins in our picture of God. The God who calls is the God who loves us and longs for us, together with the rest of all creation, to be made whole. His call will never diminish or restrict our lives. Engagement with the task to which God calls us brings us alive, releases locked up potential, and gives real fulfillment. We know we are doing what we were created for. We are speaking our message, singing our song, bestowing our act of love. We are becoming the person God wants us to be. Jesus, whose whole life was integrated around this theme of call, captures this nourishment in a memorable metaphor: "It is meat and drink for me to do the will of him who sent me until I have finished his work" (John 4:34 NEB).

But a personal call is not for our own sake alone. It continually points our heart and mind toward our neighbor, connects us with some segment of the world's pain, and meets real human need. Living out our call becomes a way in which we, like Jesus, lay down our lives on behalf of others. We become instruments of God's shalom and healing. In the words of St. Francis's prayer: Where there is hatred, we sow love; where there is injury, we bestow pardon; where there is doubt, we bring faith; where there is despair, we bring hope; where there is darkness, we shed light; where there is weakness, we inspire strength; and where there is sadness, we bring joy.

Awareness of a personal call usually evokes deep feelings of resistance. This biblical characteristic is vividly illustrated in the burning bush encounter between the God who calls and Moses. Before Moses eventually responds he seeks to sidestep his personal call with a litany of excuses. On close examination these excuses echo familiar whispers of resistance inside us all. In my rather loosely paraphrased version of Moses' five excuses you may recognize one or another of them from personal experience: "I'm nobody," "I don't know enough about God," "What happens if I fail?" "I don't have what it takes," "Someone else can do it better."

I am well acquainted with these whispers of resistance. Presently I am testing—one word at a time—what may be a calling to write. In my primary vocation as pastor I spend long hours placing words together that seek to proclaim the sacred story in a way that is fresh and faithful. I enjoy working with words and have observed their powerful effects on my life and those of others. Perhaps sensing this, one or two companions along the way have suggested that I write. Their interest has given me the courage to risk trying. But it has not lessened the forces of resistance within me. Feelings of self-doubt and inadequacy mock me constantly. I struggle to believe that I may have anything to say. The task ahead seems impossible and with Moses I want to say: "No, Lord, please use someone else."

We are not left to face these resistances alone. The God who calls also empowers us in a multitude of ways. The joy we experience in pursuing our call strengthens us. Our souls are nourished by the meat and drink that doing his will provides. Helpers mysteriously cross our paths with gifts of affirmation and encouragement. Serendipities occur that touch our lives with grace and confirm the rightness of the way we're following. For those with eyes to see and ears to hear, the word of promise given to Moses is made real for us. God is with us as he has promised and in the experiencing of this promise resistance is overcome and the call can be followed.

The biblical God calls his people into an amazing variety of tasks. A random selection of scriptural stories makes this clear: Moses invests himself in the work of people-liberation and nation-building; Isaiah proclaims an unpopular message to a stubborn people; Mary bears the Christ child into a hostile world; Joseph heeds his God-given dream and courageously protects wife and child from Herod's death squads; Simon and Andrew are invited to become fishers of men and women; Dorcas knits garments for the poor and needy; Paul builds Christ-centered faith-communities that transcend race and class. Personal calls do not come in stereotyped and standardized categories. They portray the infinite creativity of the creator-redeemer God who makes no two people alike, gifts us uniquely, and custom designs his call for you and me individually.

While amazingly varied in content these calls unite in a common cause. All serve the purposes of God's kingdom in a torn-apart and fractured world. Each person mentioned in our random selection contributed in a specific fashion, large and small, to the healing of this brokenness. Through the self-giving actions of the called person the care and compassion of Christ for people is repeatedly revealed. In some particular way, the Spirit-breathed call will, in the language of the prophet, bring good news to the oppressed, bind up the brokenhearted, proclaim liberty to captives, bring release to prisoners, and comfort those who mourn.

This feature of personal call exposes a great failing of the contemporary church. In language and life it tends to recognize one call only—the calling to the ordained ministry. I have been frequently asked by lay people about the circumstances in which my own calling to be a pastor originated. When I respond I also inquire about their experience of call. The taken-aback responses I usually receive indicate a commonly held conviction that it's only the pastor who is the called person. Nothing, as we have seen, can be further from biblical truth. Every human being has something beautiful to do for God. I have become increasingly convinced that one of my essential tasks as a pastor is the evoking of these personal callings in the lives of those in my pastoral care.

Personal calling is dynamic. This biblical feature can be traced in the life of Jesus as he went about his Father's work during the various stages of his own pilgrimage. For almost thirty years there is the

Nazareth phase of hidden preparation culminating in his baptism and wilderness choices. This is followed by the Galilean phase of public and popular ministry: leisurely walking through the countryside villages and towns, sharing meals with outcasts, feeding the hungry, healing the sick, choosing and training a band of disciples, and announcing the availability of the kingdom for all people. The Jerusalem phase with its conflict and opposition turns the spotlight in word and deed on the themes of sacrifice and suffering servanthood. Finally the resurrection phase bursts forth with its joyful work of consolation and commissioning.

Jesus teaches us that personal calling is seldom unchanging and static. I have discovered this to be true. My primary calling, as I've already written, is to pastor. As my calling has progressed, there have been clearly discernible phases. There was a lengthy period of pregnancy when I carried my call around within me. For nine years there was a time of preparation and supervision. Then I invested my energies in a decade-long task of building a local congregation. During the last three years my call has found fresh expression in three different people contexts: befriending fellow pilgrims on the Christ-following road, offering retreats and workshops that explore the signposts for this journey, and seeking to be a channel of healing for the broken and bruised. I do not know what the next phase will be. God only requires that I be open to his initiatives and responsive to his promptings.

Personal Calling and Daily Work

Unraveling the relationship strands between personal calling and daily job requires careful teasing out. The way in which the two relate varies tremendously from person to person. Generally speaking most people today would struggle to equate personal calling with what they do each day. They go to their work to earn a living and to provide for themselves and for those they love but not necessarily because of an inner sense of calling. A light story clearly makes this point. Early one morning a businessman jogging along his usual morning route finds his pathway blocked by a workman digging a ditch.

"What are you trying to do?" the jogger inquires, rather put out by the inconvenience of having to find an alternative route.

"I'm digging a ditch," replies the workman, pausing for a moment to wipe the sweat from his face.

"Why are you digging the ditch?" asks the irate jogger.

"Well," ponders the worker, "I'm digging this ditch to get the money to buy the food to get the strength to dig this ditch."

Francis Dewar, an Anglican clergyperson who runs courses and retreats to enable people to link prayer and action, has helped me enormously in clarifying this relationship between personal calling and daily job. The latter, he suggests, is accompanied by a job description, has defined expectations, and carries with it a clear role-prescription. Think of the work you do each day. Whether you are secretary or senior manager, your job is directed and defined by others. In return for doing what is required, you receive a wage. Dewar discusses the consequences of this state of affairs: "Many of us can hardly conceive what our daily activity would be if it were not *demanded* of us, *expected* of us, or at least *asked* of us by someone else."[2]

Personal calling involves living from the inside out. It is freely responding to the inner promptings of the Spirit, expressing the unique essence of who you are, and giving yourself away in some particular way that enriches the lives of others. This may be something that you do as a large or small part of your daily job; it may be an activity you pursue outside of work hours. For the growing number of unemployed and retired, personal call becomes an even more urgent issue since it often preserves a sense of personhood and dignity. Real life examples may show more clearly the different ways in which these concerns of calling and daily work are interconnected.

Three stories of friends come to mind. Through the painful death of a loved one a self-employed middle-aged man who spends his working hours doing small building alterations felt a sense of call to care for the dying. After processing his own grief over an extended length of time he applied and was accepted for a hospice care-giving course. Presently he shares in his congregation's intentional ministry to those who are dying. Amid the turmoil leading up to our country's first ever democratic elections a legal advisor in a construction company sensed a call into peacemaking. He made himself available to the local peace structures and invested his personal giftedness and skills in its work. An elderly lady retired to a small coastal resort and was moved by the loneliness of the town's many senior citizens. Each day around lunch time she makes sandwiches for two, packs them in her bag, sits down on a bench overlooking the ocean, and waits for someone to join her. When a stranger sits beside her she offers him or her a sandwich and reaches out in listening friendship.

These examples describe people living out their call without financial remuneration. We can consider ourselves extremely fortunate when personal calling and daily job coincide and we are paid for doing what we believe God is calling us to do. I think of a longtime friend who works in the area of organizational development and training. His personal calling, in his own words, is "the development of people." While his job description outlines many tasks, a large percentage of his time is given to what he believes is his life's vocation. His working hours offer him numerous opportunities to live out his inner calling. Going to work each day is an energizing and fulfilling adventure. Blessed indeed are those who are able to express their personal calling in their everyday jobs and are paid for it.

In whatever way calling and job may relate I do not want to undervalue the importance of our daily work. Finding work for which we are paid is a critical developmental task facing every young adult. This is becoming increasingly difficult. Recently a senior in high school cynically commented: "I am being educated for unemployment." Unemployment is a major soul-killing form of oppression. Last night I sat for two hours with a devastated man on the brink of suicide after he was laid off for the third time in a year. We are made in the image of the worker-God, and it is good and right for us to work. For the employed Christ-follower it is *the* place where we spend most of our adult lives learning to live our lives as he would if he were in our shoes.

Discerning and Following
One's Personal Call

Hopefully you are willing to consider the possibility that God may have something unique for you to do. You may be wondering how you can practically explore this possibility. Not every inner prompting or nudge is necessarily the voice of the Spirit. It may be the voice of culture, parents, peer pressure, or ego. Cynical stories abound of those who have claimed a call from God but whose actions have either been self-promoting or painfully destructive. Clearly there is need, not for a neat and tidy formula, but for a discerning process that enables you and me to understand the source of a call, its content, and what response is appropriate.

Personal calling implies a relationship with the One who calls. We do not manufacture or generate our own calls. They are discovered and discerned within an ever-deepening intimacy with God. In the earlier chapters of this book the signposts marking this unending spiritual journey were described: forging a Christlike picture of God, fostering a Christian memory, opening our hands to receive the kingdom, growing into fuller self-knowledge, deepening friendship bonds with fellow pilgrims, growing into the person God wants us to be, and learning to care. Walking along this signposted road places our lives consciously in the way of the God who calls, enhances our ability to discern the burning bushes across our paths, and strengthens us to act on what we have discovered. Discernment more likely occurs within the context of an active Christ-following life.

Another way of stating this is to affirm that we are called to being before we are called to doing. Jesus invites his disciples to *be* with him in community and then calls them into their ministry tasks. Communion precedes commissioning. The primary gift we bring to the world is always who we are, the compassionate and responsive person that the Spirit is gradually forming. And it is into the internal fabric of who we are becoming that God writes the special message that we are called to deliver in our lifetime. Deciphering this message is what discernment is all about. Facilitating this deciphering process are questions like: "What do I really care about?" "How can I follow my heart more faithfully?" "What are my gifts and where can they enjoy fuller expression in the cause of the kingdom?"

Personal calling intersects with the experience of pain. Perhaps this is why Paul, in that magnificent eighth chapter of the letter to the Romans, invites his readers to listen to three groans: "We know that the whole creation has been groaning. . . . Not only so, but we ourselves, who have the firstfruits of the Spirit, groan inwardly. . . . the

Spirit himself intercedes for us with groans that words cannot express" (vv. 22, 23, 26 NIV). Paying attention to these groans—in our lives and those of others—puts us in touch with the Spirit who shares our suffering, speaks to us through pain, and calls us to be channels of healing and wholeness in a broken and tormented world. Discerning our call is rooted in this kind of listening.

Attending your inner groans happens best with a trusted friend of the soul who can be your "wailing wall" and will listen prayerfully to the pain you bear. Planted there may be the buried seeds of those good deeds that God has purposed you to do. This is repeatedly witnessed in the lives of fellow travelers on the way. I am reminded of the parents of two mentally handicapped children who, in their own anguish and despair, heard the call of God to initiate a "faith and light" ministry for others in a similar position. Their pioneering efforts resulted in the forming of a small community comprising fellow parents, their handicapped children, and friends. For almost eight years they have gathered together, once every month, to celebrate their faith, share stories and struggles, and play together. Their testimony encourages us to listen to our own inner pain and seek there the clues that enable us to discern our calling.

Combined with this inner listening to your own pain there needs to be a growing awareness of the human struggles taking place in your midst. Here we recognize the critical necessity of the spiritual discipline of planned encounter with those who suffer. Through this kind of exposure there is sometimes a particular human cry that penetrates your heart more deeply than any other. In this cry you may hear God addressing you and calling you to colabor in the work of making whole what is broken. Pause for a moment and ask yourself: *What human cry in my community disturbs me the most?* Is it the cry of the dying or the bereaved? Is it the cry of the homeless poor, the drug addicted, the children of the street? Is it the cry of the depressed, the lonely, the shut-in elderly? You may discover in this cry intimations of your own calling.

Personal calling unfolds slowly. Like a person walking through a dark forest with a torch, you take one step at a time, following whatever light is given. Your own next step in exploring and following your call could include any of the following: writing down your responses to the questions suggested in this chapter, sharing your present understanding of what God may be wanting you to do with a trusted friend or group, getting more information about the area of concern to which you are drawn, sounding out your call in your local congregation and gathering others round it for future prayer and action. Whatever step you take you must always check your understanding of personal call against its biblical features mentioned earlier. Does this step nourish your own life, connect you with others, evoke some measure of resistance, serve the kingdom, and reflect the dynamic nature of call? If the answer is yes, you may be on the edge of doing something beautiful for God.

Following the Signpost Together

1. How do you respond to the statement made by Mother Teresa, "Each of us has something beautiful to do for God"?
2. Which one of the biblical features described in the chapter sheds the most light for you on the theme of personal calling?
3. How do you understand the relationship between your daily work and your calling from God?
4. What human cry in your community disturbs you the most?
5. What is your own next step in exploring and following your call?

Finding God in All Things

"inding God in all things" is a phrase that has become increasingly instructive for my own pilgrimage.[1] Constantly it enters my mind reminding me that it is within the ordinary—cooking meals, going to work, paying the bills, enjoying friendships, playing with the children—that the life of the kingdom is authentically lived. Sacred and secular cannot be separated. The presence of God is to be known where we are and in whatever we are doing.

I failed to grasp this truth in the early years of my walk with Christ. Everyday life seemed segregated into strict "spiritual" and "unspiritual" compartments. There was the sacred sphere of prayer, Bible reading, worship, and other church-related activities where God was expected to encounter one. Then there was the secular segment—those routine, mundane junctures of daily life, in my job, my family, my leisure times—which was somehow perceived to be devoid of God's active presence. Frequent exhortations by preachers to "take Christ into the world," where he was supposedly absent and nonactive, deepened this division even further.

Gradually it dawned on me that the people in the Bible saw things differently. Repeatedly the Scriptures witness to the presence of God everywhere and in everything. In his temple vision of the Lord seated high upon the throne, Isaiah speaks of the seraphim in the divine presence calling out to one another, "Holy, Holy, Holy is the LORD of hosts; the whole earth is full of his glory" (Isa. 6:3). Preaching to the Athenians, Paul declares boldly that God is always near, for "in him we live and move and have our being" (Acts 17:28). Writing later to the Ephesians he gives this truth even sharper focus: "[There is] . . . one God and Father of all, who is above all and through all and in all" (Eph. 4:6).

This way of understanding God's relationship with his world has profoundly altered my understanding of the Christ-following life. No longer is the Holy One to be encountered only within particular places, special times, and certain states of mind. His living presence pervades all things and every experience and waits only to be recognized. Wherever we may be standing—in the kitchen or at the workplace—is holy ground. We are continuously encircled and enfolded in the heart of God. Not for one second can we escape the presence of the Lord. For as the psalmist affirms, "If I went up to heaven, you would be there; if I lay down in the world of the dead, you would be there" (Ps. 139:8 TEV).

Our picture of God develops this truth further. The God in whom we live and move and have our being is the Christlike God who sacrificially and extravagantly loves every one of us. Like the shining sun that continuously sends forth its rays of light and warmth, there is no time in our lives when God is not actively loving us. His transforming love radiates toward us through every single moment and experience of our lives. This never-failing, always present love is the kingdom, the eternal realm of God that Jesus has made accessible for us now and into which we shall fully pass at the moment of our dying. Training ourselves to be aware of this glorious reality in the present moment signposts the challenge facing every Christ-follower.

This is not easy, especially for those who have suffered greatly. Not every moment is filled with sunlight. Not every experience at first glance appears to be a sacrament of God's loving presence. Not every event suggests a divine epiphany. There is an obvious conflict raging in our midst between the forces of Christ and those of darkness and evil. Oppression, poverty, torture, and pain scar the life experience of more people than we will ever know. Often the darkness can be overwhelming and we may feel that God has forgotten or forsaken us. Writing after a lifetime characterized by both immense personal pain and an intense sharing in the sufferings of others, medical doctor and author Paul Tournier observes that while some people are transformed by suffering, far more are destroyed by it.[2] We do well therefore not to speak too glibly or easily about finding God in all things.

This is also why I have found it essential to take with utmost seriousness the teachings of Jesus about the afterlife. For countless people, this earthly life has meant ongoing suffering, which has made belief in a loving God nearly impossible. This century has witnessed human misery on a scale unparalleled in human history. If this life is all there is, then it is ultimately an absurd and cruel joke. Yet, as was made clear in an earlier chapter, at the heart of the message of Jesus is the promise of the kingdom of heaven. Partially available to us now as we open our hands to receive it, this realm of infinite love and goodness will be fully known beyond the space-time dimensions of our present world. Within the endless companionship of God's presence and God's family we shall be able to become all that we're intended to be. Indeed without these eternal dimensions, the love of God is no love at all.

Numerous Christ-followers in both biblical and modern times have personally witnessed this reality of a fuller kingdom. Their testimonies encourage a vital belief in life beyond the grave. One powerful biblical example is that of Stephen, the first Christian martyr, as he was being stoned to death. In the Book of Acts we read about his experience when he gazed into heaven and saw the glory of God and Jesus standing at the right hand of God. This vision reflects the passionate conviction of the early church that *nothing* would ever be able to separate them from the love of God revealed in Jesus Christ. Little wonder this vulnerable band of disciples outlived the ancient world. They were not counting on their lives coming to a meaningless end. They understood themselves to be eternal beings living lives that would never cease to be. They took with absolute seriousness the assurance of Jesus that those who kept his word would never see death (see John 8:51).

Recently I came across a very moving written testimony in which the widely respected theologian and writer Henri Nouwen shares his glimpse into God's eternal realm. On a dark winter's morning in 1988 he experienced a nearly fatal accident that brought him into that shadowland between life and death and also led him into a new experience of God. In his remarkable little book *Beyond the Mirror* he describes this experience within the portal of death. He writes:

What I experienced then was something I had never experienced before: pure and unconditional love. Better still, what I experienced was an intensely personal presence, a presence that pushed all my fears aside and said, "Come, don't be afraid. I love you." A very gentle, nonjudgmental presence; a presence that simply asked me to trust and trust completely . . . I had spent countless hours studying the Scriptures, listening to lectures and sermons, and reading spiritual books. Jesus had been very close to me, but also very distant; a friend, but also a stranger; a source of hope, but also of fear, guilt and shame. But now, when I walked around the portal of death, all ambiguity and all uncertainty were gone. He was there, the Lord of my life, saying, "Come to me, come."

A few paragraphs later he continues:

This experience was the realisation of my oldest and deepest desires. Since the first moment of consciousness, I have had the desire to be with Jesus. Now I felt his presence in a most tangible way, as if my whole life had come together and I was being enfolded in love.[3]

Only those empowered by this kingdom hope will venture forth and experiment with a training program designed to find God in all things. The kingdom of God is made accessible through the presence of the crucified-risen Christ, and this presence needs to be invoked in order for us to experience the kingdom. How we go about invoking the divine presence is what is meant by a training program. One possibility consists of three closely related and user-friendly practices: turning the mind regularly in a Christward direction, keeping constantly thankful, and doing everything we do for God. Finding their origins in the wisdom of Scripture, these practices have been explored in the great spiritual classics and are accessible to us all. For those who live busy, active, and filled lives, an extra plus is that they demand no additional time commitments away from family or work.

In recent years I have experimented with these practices within the nitty-gritty of my own daily routines and relationships. In spite of frequent lapses and having constantly to restart the program, they have become the channel for numerous blessings. These range from receiving strength and help in times of difficulty to a far broader awareness of God's active presence in commonplace occasions and duties. Without engagement in practices like these I am convinced that we shall not cultivate a sense of the holy amid the ordinary.

Turning the Mind in a Christward Direction

The Greek word for repentance makes it clear that access to the Holy One occurs primarily through the mind. *Metanoia* describes the radical change in thinking style that accompanies genuine conversion. Quite literally it means "thinking about our thinking." Whereas previous to conversion we lived our lives without reference to Christ, there is now the desire to let him be the center of our thinking and living. Regularly turning our minds toward him is one practical way of ensuring that this happens.

This does not mean thinking *only* about the Holy One all the time. This could have disastrous consequences concerning the tasks we have to accomplish. I like the story that David Sheppard, Bishop of Liverpool, tells about himself. He was playing in a crucial championship cricket match between Australia and England. He had recently been ordained as a priest. In the outfield he dropped a vital catch. An Australian spectator shouted at him from the stands, "Hey, parson, keep your eye on the ball and take your mind off God."

We direct the mind Christward by frequently affirming the nearbyness of the divine presence. Whether washing dishes, doing housework, sitting in the boardroom, working on the factory floor, or typing reports, we acknowledge that God is with us wherever we are. These repeated affirmations may find their shape in a short prayer inwardly whispered, a biblical phrase recalled, a silent pause. Sometimes just repeating the name of Jesus centers our lives in that portable inner sanctuary where the Most High dwells. This way of invoking the presence of Christ is made known through an easy to read little book called *The Way of the Pilgrim*. It tells the story of a Russian peasant and pilgrim who repeated the name of Jesus wherever he went and it describes the experiences that resulted from this practice.

With these little affirmations we are not trying to generate or manufacture the presence of God. The bottom line has already been clearly established: in God we live and move and have our being. Or as Paul elsewhere reflects: "In him all things hold together" (Col. 1:17). Developing the practice of this mental habit takes this truth seriously and acts boldly on it. There come times when dark circumstances, painful relationships, and feelings of spiritual barrenness will mock our attempts at this practice. In such moments continuing with our affirmations demonstrates a trusting faith that there is nothing "able to separate us from the love of God in Christ Jesus our Lord" (Rom. 8:39).

This simple practice yields life-transforming benefits. In his personal journal written while he labored as a missionary in the southern Philippines, Frank Laubach describes the results of his holy experiment with God. On the third of January 1930 he resolved to direct his mind Godward for one second out of every minute. Twenty-nine days later he made the following journal entry:

> The sense of being led by an unseen hand which takes mine, while another hand reaches ahead and prepares the way, grows upon me daily. I do not need to strain at all to find opportunity. It piles in upon me as waves roll over the beach, and yet there is time to do something about each opportunity. . . . I feel, I *feel* like one who has had his violin out of tune with the orchestra and at last is in harmony with the music of the universe.[4]

Habits of holy mindfulness are not easily formed. In their awkward early stages they need all the help they can get. Tangible symbols of the holy help us in this regard. Orthodox Russian believers place an icon in the corner of each room, which communicates a sense of the sacred to anyone who enters. A business executive friend of mine writes out a Bible verse on his desktop pad. A housewife I know plays a music tape of Taize chants while she dusts and sweeps. Can you think of some external sign that, if strategically placed in your home or place of work, would encourage you to be more mindful of God's nearby presence?

You and I can begin experimenting with this practice immediately. Decide on the shape of your little affirmation. Is it going to be a short prayer, a favorite

Scripture verse, the loving repetition of the name of Jesus? Begin to use it right now. Refuse to be discouraged by what Quaker Thomas Kelly calls frequent "lapses and forgettings." Without self-accusation, gently remind yourself of your intentions and begin again just where you are. After a period of experimentation reflect on the experience and see whether your relationship with God and awareness of the divine presence has been deepened.

Keeping Constantly Thankful

Choosing to remain constantly thankful nurtures the awareness of God's immediate presence. This could be one reason why thanksgiving is central to biblical prayer. Throughout Scripture we receive repeated invitations to grow in the way of gratitude. Tucked away in Paul's first letter to the Thessalonians is one of these invitations. Crammed with wise insight it reads: "Be joyful always; pray continually; be thankful in all circumstances, for this is God's will for you in Christ Jesus" (1 Thess. 5:17–18 NIV).

By addressing his words to the wills of his readers Paul assumes that gratitude is a choice. In whatever circumstance we find ourselves we are given the freedom to choose our response. Particularly in painful and difficult circumstances we can ask, as Baptist minister and author John Claypool has pointed out, the resentment question—*Why did this have to happen to me?*—and focus on the negative. Or we can ask the gratitude question—*What is there here to be thankful for that can be used in constructing a new future?*—and focus on the positive. The first choice leads us into despair and paralysis while the latter increases our sense of God's presence and results in courageous and victorious living.

Pastor Claypool makes his point, not from an academic ivory tower, but from within the crucible of personal suffering and grief. At the tender age of ten, Laura Lue, his daughter, died from acute leukemia. In the desolate days following her death he wrestled with bitter resentment and despair. "What kind of God are you?" he raged. "Why did you allow an innocent little girl to suffer as she did and then die? What right did you have to take away the one I cherished?"

Claypool chose, however, not to travel down the road of resentment. With what must have been immense courage he asked himself the gratitude question and answered:

> Who was Laura Lue, really? She had been a gift—not something I had created and therefore had the right to clutch as an owned possession, but a treasure who had always belonged to Another.

She had been with me solely through the gracious generosity of that One. . . . At every given juncture, we humans are given the freedom to choose the attitudes we assume, and so it was with me. I could be angry that Laura Lue had died after only ten short years, or I could be grateful that she had lived at all and that I had been able to share in her wonder. I chose then, and I still do, the way of gratitude.[5]

I quote John Claypool's experience at length for his words stir the heart and mind. They teach us that gratitude is not a dutiful obligation—it is an appropriate response to the sheer giftedness of our lives. What do we have that has not ultimately been given? Awakening to this truth releases the flow of gratitude and thankfulness. Nothing is taken for granted anymore. Our posture toward life shifts from grabbing, demanding, and complaining to one of receiving, celebrating, and delighting. Everywhere and in everything the goodness of God is seen—in every warm embrace we receive, every drink of water we take, every mouthful of food we eat. When we are caught up in the immeasurable grace and generosity of the giver, the sense of God's presence in all things is enhanced and deepened.

We can decide to embark on this way of gratitude immediately. Delight in those small rituals of everyday life that are usually taken for granted. This could mean enjoying a walk around the block, eating slowly, or just lingering over a cup of coffee. Fill the day with gestures of thankfulness—saying thank-you, writing notes of appreciation, giving a hug. Pause at regular intervals to give thanks to God for every sign of his goodness. Thank the Holy One for gifts of sleep and rest, food and work, friends and family. In all these good gifts God is present, pouring himself out in self-giving love for us to receive and enjoy.

Doing Everything for God

An ancient story goes as follows: Three masons were building a cathedral. When asked about what they were doing, the first mason answered, "I am putting one stone upon another in order to build a wall." The second mason said, "I am working so that I can purchase food and clothing for myself and my family." But the third mason replied, "I am building a house of God so that people may know God's presence and be joyful."

Three attitudes toward everyday tasks and occupations are reflected in this simple story. We can live and work mechanically, putting one stone on the other, day after day, until the wall is built; or we can live and work solely for ourselves and our loved ones without thought for others and their needs; or we can offer up our daily work to

God, whether it be washing dishes or selling insurance or being a doctor, and so build a world in which the divine presence is made manifest and where people can find joy.

Dare we adopt this last attitude toward those mundane and unspectacular tasks that fill our lives? Ninety percent of what we do every day bears little overt religious significance. Think for a moment through your own daily schedule. Make a mental list of those routine and regular tasks that occupy most of your waking time. If my hunch is accurate, most of these activities are neither very pious or churchy. We wake up, go about our jobs either at home or in the workplace, have our meals, enjoy some leisure moments with friends and family, and retire to bed. Yet it is my firm belief that Paul had tasks like these in mind when he offered the following nugget of spiritual direction to the Corinthian church: "So whether you eat or drink or whatever you do, do it all for the glory of God" (1 Cor. 10:31 NIV).

The ordinary is made holy when we resolve to do everything we do for God. Brother Lawrence models what this may mean for us. For fifteen years amid the hustle and bustle of a monastery's kitchen this semiliterate Christ-follower endeavored to live and work with a constant sense of God's presence. One of the ways through which he sought to realize the presence of God was to direct all his actions to God's glory. Nothing was too trivial or ordinary. Whether it was baking pancakes or picking straws off the floor, he sought to do everything for the sake of his king. Abbe de Beaufort, who edited his conversations and letters, provides us with a glimpse of Brother Lawrence at work: "And it was observed, that in the greatest hurry of business in the kitchen, he still preserved his recollection and heavenly mindedness. He was never hasty nor loitering, but did each thing in its season, with an even, uninterrupted composure and tranquility of spirit."[6]

To do everything for God is to put your whole heart into whatever you are doing in the present moment. Imagine the difference such wholehearted living would make to the quality and meaningfulness of your daily labor. I like the Hasidic story about a devout rabbi who was known to have lived an unusually fulfilled and abundant life. After his death one of his pupils was asked, "What was most important to your teacher?" Without hesitation the pupil answered, "Whatever he happened to be doing at the moment."

Wholehearted living eludes many of us. Preoccupied with external demands and internal pressures we find it hard to concentrate on the task at hand. The more routine and menial the task the harder it is to be fully present. Before we realize it our attention drifts someplace else and no longer are we attentive to what is before us. This happened to me in a recent counseling experience. While listening to a distraught man I suddenly caught myself anxiously wondering how I was going to meet the fast approaching deadline for the completion of this manuscript! Doing one thing and thinking of another is a sure sign of a scattered and halfhearted way of living.

Help is needed from beyond ourselves if we are going to engage the present task with the whole of our hearts. Consciously welcoming the Holy One into every new activity before we begin it opens our lives to this aid. Invoking God's presence into our work enables us to do it differently. We become present where we are and more focused on what we are about to do. There is given to us a deepened sensitivity to the sacredness of the now-moment and to the ethical challenges it may present. Certainly this was my experience in the above counseling encounter. When I realized that I had disengaged from the present moment, I immediately asked for help. *Lord,* I inwardly prayed, *please help me to put my preoccupations to one side and to bear your listening love to this man.* Within seconds I felt myself reestablished in God's presence and I was genuinely able to do what I was doing for his sake.

Since we are exploring the *practice* of the presence of God let me suggest another holy experiment. In a few moments you will complete your reading of this chapter and move on to your next task. Before you begin, welcome the Holy One into whatever you are about to do. Say something like, "With your help, Lord, I commit myself now to the task of playing with the children," or "With your help, Lord, I want to be present to my spouse," or "With your help I want to give myself to the task of writing this letter." After your brief prayer give yourself wholeheartedly to your planned task. Resolve inwardly not only to do it with God but also for God.

In summary, the Holy One comes to us in every moment of our lives and in every task we do. Christ, crucified and risen, meets us wherever we live and work and play. Precisely here, amid the ordinary and commonplace, the life of the kingdom is made available. Turning the mind in a Christward direction, keeping constantly thankful, and doing everything for God constitute a faithful response to this good news. Through practices like these, daily life is integrated into the kingdom, the divine presence is known in all things, and everyday life becomes for you and me nothing less than "the house of God; . . . the gate of heaven" (Gen. 28:17).

Following the Signpost Together

1. How would you describe your experience of God amid the routines of your everyday life?
2. Share your attempts to remain aware of God's presence during the day. What do you find most helpful?
3. When in difficult and painful circumstances do you tend to ask the resentment question or the gratitude question? Discuss your responses.
4. How would daily life be different if you sought to offer everything you did to God?
5. Select one way of deepening your awareness of God's presence in your everyday life in the coming days and share this resolve with your group.

Growing into Christlikeness

O nce I participated in a group discussion where we were asked to design a motto that would most faithfully describe the life and ministry of Jesus. "People matter" were the two words that I chose. From beginning to end the actions and sayings of Jesus are characterized by a profound and passionate concern for people. Understanding this supreme gospel value signposts our way forward toward the goal of the Christ-following life.

This goal can be simply stated: *To be a disciple of Jesus is to grow into Christlikeness.* In his letters Paul constantly encourages his readers to press toward this goal. Maturity in discipleship involves putting on Christ, becoming like him, and sharing in his nature.[1] Clarity in this matter focuses the overall direction for the Christ-following life, saves us from falling prey to the latest fads and fashions in the spiritual supermarket, and keeps our spirituality in faithful relationship with the spirit of the crucified-risen Lord.

But what does it mean to be like Christ? We can find out. Trace the footsteps of Jesus through the Gospels. Listen to him teach the meaning of kingdom living. Observe him carefully in his ministry encounters with everyday women and men. People matter more than anything else. Jesus recognized the image of God in every human being. With uncanny double vision he sees people as they are and as they can become. Seeing people through these eyes he both enfleshes the heart of the Holy One and demonstrates the intended outcome of his transforming work in our lives.

From God's perspective there is nothing more valuable than the human being. Right from the outset of the biblical record this is made clear. In the first chapter of the Bible we discover that, of the entire created order, only you and I bear the divine image. A few sentences later we learn that it is into human hands that God entrusts the responsibility for his world. Reflecting on this rather awesome job description the stargazing psalmist exclaims with wonder that we have been made "little lower than God, and crowned . . . with glory and honor" (Ps. 8:5). Can we see how much we really matter?

God's attitude toward human life becomes audible and visible in the life and ministry of Jesus. Listen in on his conversation with his disciples as he draws a comparison between people and the birds of the air: "Are not five sparrows sold for two pennies? Yet not one of them is forgotten in God's sight. But even the hairs of your head are all counted. Do not be afraid; you are of more value than many sparrows" (Luke 12:6). Imagine the life-affirming effect these words would have had on the lives of these early Christ-followers. Without a shadow of doubt they would have known that they mattered to Jesus and to the One of whom he spoke.

Sayings like these were underlined by the actions of Jesus. Whether it was hugging a little child nagging for attention, touching an outcast leper living in the margins of society, sitting down for a meal with a politically incorrect tax collector, or affirming a used and abused prostitute, Jesus acted toward individuals with immeasurable respect and care. He enabled them to realize their sacredness and specialness. He called forth from their depths their very best. People mattered to Jesus more than they would ever fully comprehend and he loves them—and us—to the end.

This is the heart that Jesus desires to form in us. Recall that gospel invitation extended by Jesus to the two fishermen, Simon and his brother Andrew, as they cast their nets into the Sea of Galilee. "Follow me," says Jesus, "and I will make you fish for people" (Mark 1:17). For many years I interpreted these words in a strict evangelical sense. Here, I believed, Jesus was seeking to motivate his disciples into "catching people" for the kingdom. Only after spending a few hours in the company of a committed fisherman did I reconsider my understanding of this text.

Fishermen, I discovered, are passionate people passionate about fish! They prepare for their fishing adventures with painstaking attention, rise from sleep at unearthly hours, fish throughout night and day with enduring patience, and, on arriving home, talk incessantly about their triumphs and near triumphs! Their hearts are set on the task of fishing. Knowing this to be true about Simon and Andrew, Jesus in effect says to them: Come with me and I will replace your passion for fish with another kind. I will form in your heart the divine passion for people. You will learn to see men and women through my eyes.

This learning to see people differently takes time. Certainly this has been true of my own experience. Over the years the poverty of my own eyesight has revealed itself in a variety of ways: cynicism and resentment toward people's needs, nonresponsiveness in the face of visible suffering, lack of engagement with those principalities and powers that have sought to dominate and oppress, and sometimes personal actions and words that I know have brought harm to others. Still today, in spite of really wanting to see people through the eyes of Jesus, these symptoms of dull vision constantly reappear.

Regularly checking the eyes of one's heart is therefore a gospel necessity. For this diagnostic exercise you may want to search out your responses to the following questions: With what kind of eyes do I see people? Is my seeing prejudiced by the other person's color or culture? In relation to my neighbor's pain do I have eyes that are aware or blind? Do I see people as mere statistics or, as Archbishop Desmond Tutu once said, "sacraments of God's presence"? Wrestling with questions like these is crucial for the serious Christ-follower. For the way we see others determines the way we behave and relate to one another.

A legend from the Middle Ages makes this clear: Two warriors in full armor were riding along in a forest, each thinking he was alone. In a particularly dark and wooded area their paths crossed. Both were frightened and each interpreted the movements of the other as hostile. Believing they were in danger for their lives the knights unbuckled their weapons and began to fight. When the one knight fell to the ground the other rode across to him and drove his lance through his heart. The victor dismounted and walked over to the one he had killed. He pulled back the face mask and there to his horror in the pale moonlight he recognized his own brother. Faulty seeing had ended in tragedy.

In our blindness we hurt and destroy each other. That is the story of our lives and of our world. Like the blind man of Bethsaida we desperately need the second touch of Jesus. Remember how after Jesus had placed saliva on the blind man's eyes and touched him, he asked the man, "Can you see anything?" "I can see people but they look like trees walking," the man replied. And then Jesus touched the man a second time and he was able to see everyone clearly (Mark 8:23–25). This blind man symbolizes our common need for a fresh way of seeing. *Lord Jesus,* our cry must be, *help me see that people matter. Enable me to recognize your image in all men and women. Form your divine passion for people in my heart. And may all that I do and say spring from this supreme value of yours.*

Integrating this supreme gospel value into the fabric of our inner being requires determined effort. Apostle Paul again proves to be an insightful spiritual guide. Repeatedly he reminds us that personal transformation will not happen without our whole-hearted cooperation. His writings are peppered with phrases inviting us to participate with the Spirit in our ongoing conversion: "Put away your former way of life"; "clothe yourself with the new self"; "put on the Lord Jesus"; and "above all, clothe yourselves with love."[2] Discerning those behaviors that are characteristic of Jesus and making them our own is one way of taking these invitations seriously. From my own reflections I propose three "gospel actions" as a starting point. From your own reading of the Gospels, you may want to revise and add to the list.

The Gospel Action of Hospitality

In our communion liturgy there is a grace-filled moment when, immediately after the bread and wine have been consecrated, the minister turns to the congregation and says: "This is the Lord's table. Christ is our host and he invites all to come and feast." There can be no more vivid symbol of the gracious hospitality that God extends to his people. Everyone's name appears on the invitation list for the banquet of the kingdom. There is a place especially reserved for you and me. The testimony of the psalmist becomes our own: "He prepares a table before me" (Ps. 23:5).

Not surprisingly, therefore, both Jesus and his early followers practiced hospitality. You will have gleaned from your own reading of the Gospels that whenever Jesus was at table anybody and everybody was welcome. Nobody was sent away. This was the scandal that horrified the religious leaders, challenged prevailing customs, but—on the other hand—made the gospel credible for those outsiders and outcasts who felt they did not matter. Later the theme of hospitality would appear in the writings of both Peter and Paul and became in the expansion of the church one of the key criteria for holding a position of leadership in the local congregation.

Hospitality gets twisted these days to serve ends that betray its essential nature. Sometimes the outwardly hospitable invitation disguises a multitude of less attractive hidden agendas. Have you ever had the experience when, at the conclusion of an evening shared with your hosts, you wondered why they wanted your company in the first place? Was your presence desired because your hosts honestly cared about you and wanted to get to know you—or was it a calculated effort toward getting what they needed from you? When I was talking about this kind of hospitality abuse with a friend the other day he made a comment that echoed something of my own suspicions. "Hospitality," he remarked, "has become a subtle and sophisticated form of social engineering."

Nothing could be further from what genuine hospitality is all about. Read again about Abraham receiving three strangers at Mamre and giving them water, bread, and meat (Gen. 18:1–15); the widow of Zarephath offering food and shelter to Elijah (1 Kings 17:9–24); and of the two Emmaus pilgrims inviting the stranger home with them to sleep over for the night (Luke 24:13–35). From these biblical stories we learn that hospitality is a way of saying to another, "You matter. I welcome you and want to provide you a safe place where you can be yourself. If at all possible I will meet your needs for friendship and refreshment. I have no desire to change you or get anything from you. Make yourself at home."

Often it is the poor who teach us most about hospitality. Some years ago on a Pilgrimage of Pain and Hope we spent three days sharing the life of a deprived and dispossessed community. Two of the pilgrims, both young women in their early twenties, lived with a family of six in a two-room dwelling. For the duration of their stay the husband and wife insisted that the two pilgrims use their bed while they themselves slept on the floor in the adjoining room with their children. Each morning they found that water had been heated for them over an open fire and a breakfast cooked. When they left they were given a small gift to take with them back to their families.

Our next stay was in an exclusive and affluent suburb of a major South African city. The same two pilgrims were placed with a couple living alone in a two-story home. When they arrived, the young adults were asked if they would use their sleeping bags and sleep on the carpet in the family room. Breakfast was cooked for them by the domestic worker, left on the kitchen table, and eaten alone without their hosts. On the last day of their stay you can imagine the shock and surprise for these pilgrims when they discovered upstairs three unused, furnished bedrooms. Their contrasting experience became for all of us on that pilgrimage a powerful lesson in generous and costly hospitality.

Hospitality takes place in a variety of ways and on many different levels. Henri Nouwen suggests that parents offer hospitality to their children when they provide a free and friendly space for them in which they can grow and become their own persons.[3] We extend hospitality by asking friends and those who are still strangers to come and share a meal. It may involve including in our circle of friends the outsider in our midst, serenely accepting an interruption by a visitor, or welcoming a newcomer at our place of work. Yesterday it meant for me approaching a stranger in our parking lot and asking if I could help him in any way. "Yes," he replied, "I have inoperable cancer and need some space to pray." I invited him into our chapel where we sat in the silence together. However it may happen, hospitality is a sign of that great banquet to which all have been invited and where everyone matters.

The Gospel Action of Loving Our Enemies

Return again to our picture of God provided by Jesus through his words and deeds. In his teaching on the mountainside Jesus articulates for his followers what is self-evident from the world of nature. Clearly the Holy One is not someone who rewards the good with sunshine and rain and

punishes the wicked with drought and disaster.
Experience teaches us that he "makes his sun rise
on the evil and on the good, and sends rain on the
righteous and on the unrighteous" (Matt. 5:45).
He treats friend and foe alike. The blessedness of
the kingdom is made available to anyone, even
the enemy of God, who wants to enter.

God's indiscriminate and all-inclusive love
embodies itself vividly in the actions of Jesus. The
writers of the various Gospels make it obvious that
there were many who despised Jesus and wanted
to do away with him. Yet at no point throughout
his public ministry does he seek their exclusion
from the goodness and mercy of the One by
whom he had been sent. Even from the agony and
anguish of the cross Jesus cries out for the Father's
blessing on those who planned his death. "For-
give them," he prays, "for they do not know what
they are doing" (Luke 23:34).

Bringing our lives into sync with this surprising kind of God requires that we relate to our enemies in a similar spirit. There is no way around
this difficult challenge. We are to love our enemies, commands Jesus, because this is what God
does. The early church took these words seriously.
Indeed it was this attitude toward the enemy that
constituted one of the major ingredients of their
radical witness for the gospel. Recall for a moment
the prayer that Stephen, the first Christ-following

martyr, offers up to God as he is being stoned to death. We can almost hear the Spirit of Jesus speaking through him. "Lord," he cries out on behalf of his persecutors, "do not hold this sin against them" (Acts 7:60).

How on earth do we begin to love the enemy? Acknowledging who they are and our real feelings toward them chalks out the starting line. It is a fact that all of us have enemies. It could be someone within the family, a neighbor across the street, a colleague in the workplace, or someone we consider an oppressor or exploiter. Enemies are those to whom we feel hostile and who sometimes feel hostile toward us. They are the people we try to avoid, speak negatively about in their absence, or just cannot stand. Usually we feel that they have sinned against us in one way or another. Unless we honestly own the truth that there are people against whom we harbor feelings of hostility and vengeance we shall remain stuck in our relationships with them.

Refusing to retaliate keeps alive the potential for redeeming every relationship. Knowing what such refusal does *not* mean is critical. New Testament scholar Walter Wink, in his careful exploration of the nonretaliation emphasis in the life of Jesus, insists that it does not suggest submission to evil or passivity in the face of injustice. Loving enemies sometimes requires tough confrontation. He cites the situation of a battered wife whose husband has become the enemy. The most loving thing she might do would be to have her husband arrested. This would bring the issue into the open, put the abuser under a court order that would mean jail if the abuse continued, and potentially begin a process that would not only deliver the woman from being battered, but free the man from battering as well.[4]

Through his own responses to those who made themselves his enemies, Jesus discloses the essence of nonretaliation. Turning the other cheek, giving your cloak away, and going the second mile imply a refusal to be violent toward our enemies. At its most basic—and hardest—level this involves not speaking negatively or critically about them behind their backs. Gossip is a deadly form of violence—it damages our own spirits, builds a climate of suspicion and mistrust, and injures the other person's reputation without his being able to defend himself. If we do have to speak about another person unkindly, either because of the intensity of our own hurt or the possibilities of further damage being caused to others, this speaking must happen in the presence of the person concerned or within the appropriate professional context.

Prayer for one's enemies that results in practical action for their good is a further step toward loving them. Have you not discovered from personal experience that when you pray for someone whom you dislike, you begin to view that person in a fresh light? From this new way of seeing there flows a new way of relating. If you are skeptical about this, you may want to risk yourself in another experiment: Think of someone from whom you are presently estranged. Own your feelings toward that person and offer him or her honestly to God. Resolve to halt all unkind talk about this person in his or her absence. Hold him or her in the light of God's presence and pray for the person's blessing and enrichment. Finally, ask the Spirit to guide you into some practical expression of love on his or her behalf. Observe the effects of the experiment on your relationship both with the Holy One and with the person concerned.

The Gospel Action of Doing Good

Unlike some modern-day followers, Jesus would have had no problem with being called a do-gooder! Indeed it was one of the ways in which those who knew him well interpreted his actions. In his reflections, Luke writes that Jesus was "a good man, full of the Holy Spirit and faith" (Acts 11:24) who "went about doing good" (10:38). Whenever this gospel action has marked the spirituality of his followers there has been a significant impact on the life-texture of the surrounding community.

The transforming effect that those caught up in the great Wesleyan Revival exercised on eighteenth-century England is one prominent example. As John Wesley preached men and women into the kingdom, he simultaneously challenged them to bring an oppressive and decaying society into conformity with that kingdom. His converts rose to the challenge of the historical moment. Commenting on their efforts, leading South African churchperson Bishop Peter Storey points out that the "first co-operatives, the beginnings of social work, the liberation of slaves, the emancipation of labour, popular education, the Trade Union movement; all of these and more were established by the spiritual descendants of Wesley."[5] The secret underlying their astonishing witness lay in their passionate commitment to this one gospel action. On a weekly basis all members of the Wesleyan movement were enjoined "to avoid evil, to do no harm and to do *all the good* (my italics) they could for as many as possible."[6]

At our peril, we overlook the lesson implied in this historical example. Disorganized good offers weak opposition to organized evil. Personal concerns for good, if they are going to effectively counter institutional evil, must be corporately organized for creative action. During the period of the church's struggle against legalized apartheid this same lesson was learned by many Christ-followers in South Africa. This highly sophisticated and structured evil necessitated much greater opposition than isolated acts of personal goodness could offer—it required the disciplined commitment of organized intercession, organized protest, and organized resistance. With this struggle now thankfully in the past the present tasks of national reconstruction and development will demand from us an ongoing commitment to organized efforts for good.

Alongside this participation in organized movements for good there is the ever-present challenge to spontaneously fill our everyday encounters with as much personal goodness as possible. Opportunities abound in almost every situation in which we find ourselves. We can stop lying and begin speaking the truth. We can offer practical assistance to others in those seemingly trivial and trifling tasks of daily living. We can respect the rituals of courtesy that are found in every culture. Saying thank-you, writing letters of appreciation, and answering phone messages are all small actions that affirm the dignity of those with whom we regularly interact. Archbishop Tutu testifies to the indelible impression left on his memory when, as a young boy growing up in apartheid South Africa, he witnessed an elderly white priest raising his hat in greeting to Tutu's aging mother.

Individual actions for good stand out as bright stars in a dark sky. Their witness value for the kingdom cannot be measured in temporal terms. I realized this again when reading a magazine article describing the frightening levels of violence and immorality in present-day South African society. One incident witnessed by the journalist had kept him from complete cynicism and despair. Taking place amid a protest march that had erupted into an orgy of public looting and indiscriminate violence, it consisted of a single action by a lone woman marcher. While the angry marchers had begun to smash windows and help themselves to the displayed goods this woman refused to participate. Standing outside the shattered windows of a large department store, she kept shouting, almost crying out in frustration: "Stop it, comrades. Discipline. Don't give us a bad name!" For a moment, writes Rian Malan, it seemed as if the looters were going to attack her, but she stood her ground, and they melted away. She was left holding a single shoe, some marcher having disappeared with its partner. Then she reached through the shattered window and returned it to its proper place.[7]

I do not know this anonymous and courageous woman. Her action was not headlined in the popular press, filmed for national television, or rewarded by public acclaim. But it reached deep into a despairing journalist's heart and, through his written words, shed rays of light and hope on the hearts of many readers including my own. Her simple deed exemplifies the kind of light-bearing power that accompanies the gospel action of doing good. Imagine, if you will, the transforming effect that thousands of Christ-followers distributed throughout society could have on social and political structures if they, like this lone woman, could be counted on not to cooperate with evil but instead to do what is good.

These three gospel actions, and others like them, embody God's compassionate concern for those near us and enable them to believe that they really do matter. A loud warning bell must be sounded, however. Embarking on this set of behaviors without the inward guiding and empowering presence of the Spirit will surely result in legalism and burnout. Openness to the spiritual resources and energies of the kingdom is an absolute necessity. And these will become ours only as we engage these gospel actions in loving reliance on the ever-present crucified and risen Christ. "If you love me, you will keep my commandments," he said, "and I will ask the Father, and he will give you another Advocate, to be with you forever" (John 14:15).

You and I are called to become like Christ. This goal for the Christ-following life coincides with the desperate needs and challenges of our contemporary world. The times cry out for an unstoppable and sweeping movement of Christlikeness throughout the earth. Nothing else will keep human life sacred. Learning to live our lives as Jesus would if he were living in our place is not simply the most important thing in our lives; it is the only thing. May we journey single-mindedly toward this goal and may the signposts outlined in these pages guide us on the way.

Following the Signpost Together

1. What motto would you give to the life of Jesus?
2. Share one experience of receiving hospitality that meant a great deal to you.
3. How do you feel about the nonretaliation emphasis in the teachings of Jesus?
4. "Disorganized good offers weak opposition to organized evil." Discuss this statement.
5. What are your plans to grow into Christ-likeness?

Notes

Drawing a Picture of God

1. William Barclay, *Testament of Faith* (London & Oxford: Mowbrays, 1975), 46.

2. James Houston, *The Transforming Friendship* (Batavia, Ill.: Lion Publishing, 1989), 216.

3. John Powell, *The Christian Vision* (Allen, Tex.: Tabor, 1984), 94.

4. Albert Nolan, *Jesus before Christianity* (Maryknoll, N.Y.: Orbis Books, 1978), 39.

5. Alan Jones, *Passion for Pilgrimage* (San Francisco: Harper & Row, 1989), 105.

Developing a Christian Memory

1. Joseph Girzone, *Never Alone* (Dublin: Gill and Macmillan Ltd., 1994), 7.

2. Henri Nouwen, *The Living Reminder* (Minneapolis: Seabury Press, 1977), 22.

3. If you are interested in exploring the ideas of Ignatius for the present day I would recommend *Finding God in All Things* by Margaret Heloblethwaite (London: Fount Paperbacks, 1987).

Receiving the Kingdom

1. Girzone, *Never Alone*, 63.

2. William Temple, *Readings in St John's Gospel* (London: Macmillan, 1963), 24.

3. See Donald English, *Why Believe in Jesus* (London: Epworth Press, 1986).

Acknowledging Our Shadow Selves

1. Elizabeth O'Connor, *Our Many Selves* (New York: Harper and Row, 1971), 3.

2. William Miller, *The Joy of Feeling Good* (Minneapolis: Augsburg, 1986), 83.

3. Elizabeth O'Connor outlines a similar exercise in her book *Our Many Selves*, 43.

4. Walter Wink, *Engaging the Powers* (Minneapolis: Augsburg, 1992), 273.

5. Morton Kelsey, *Adventure Inward* (Minneapolis: Augsburg, 1980), 192.

Belonging to the Family of God

1. Interview with Cheryl Carolus in *The Spirit of Hope,* ed. Charles Villa-Vicencio (Johannesburg: Skotaville Publishers, 1993), 56.

2. See Romans 15:7; John 15:12; 13:14.

3. Interview with Mmutlanyane Mogoba in *The Spirit of Hope,* 197.

4. More information can be obtained about gospel-sharing groups and other methods of gospel sharing from Lumko Institute, P.O. Box 5058, Delmenville 1403, South Africa.

Becoming Holy, Becoming Ourselves

1. Donald McCullough, *Waking from the American Dream* (Downers Grove, Ill.: InterVarsity Press, 1988), 101.

2. The two most helpful books that I have found on this subject are Richard Foster, *The Celebration of Discipline* (New York: Harper and Row, 1978), and Dallas Willard, *The Spirit of the Disciplines* (New York: Harper and Row, 1988).

3. Donald Nicholl, *Holiness* (London: Darton, Longman & Todd Ltd., 1981), 62.

4. I first came across this story in Henri Boulad's *All Is Grace* (London: SCM Press, 1991).

5. Kenneth Leech writes of "the culture of false inwardness" in *The Eye of the Storm* (London: Darton, Longman & Todd Ltd., 1992), 14.

Loving Those Closest to Us

1. Elton Trueblood, "Quarterly Yoke Letter," June 1994.

2. Morton T. Kelsey, *Caring* (New York: Paulist Press, 1981), 65.

3. For a fuller exploration into the activity of listening, I warmly recommend *Listening* by Anne Long (London: Daybreak DLT, 1990).

4. Dietrich Bonhoeffer, *Life Together* (London: SCM Press, 1954), 87.

Discovering God's Call for Our Lives

1. I came across this ancient Christian tradition in John Powell's *Through Seasons of the Heart* (London: Fount Paperbacks, 1987), 373.

2. Francis Dewar, *Called or Collared?* (London: SPCK, 1991), 6.

Finding God in All Things

1. "Finding God in all things" is a phrase usually associated with Ignatian spirituality.

2. See Paul Tournier's *Creative Suffering* (London: SCM Press, 1982).

3. Henri J. M. Nouwen, *Beyond the Mirror* (New York: Crossroad, 1990), 35, 37.

4. Frank C. Laubach, *Open Windows, Swinging Doors* (Ventura, Calif.: Regal, 1955), 17.

5. John Claypool, *Opening Blind Eyes* (Nashville: Abingdon Press, 1983), 69 (quoted with author's permission).

6. Brother Lawrence, *The Practice of the Presence of God* (London: Samuel Bagster & Sons Ltd.), 37.

Growing into Christlikeness

1. See passages like Galatians 3:17; 2 Corinthians 3:18; Galatians 4:19; and Philippians 2:5.

2. See passages like Colossians 3:9–10; Galatians 3:27; and Colossians 3:14.

3. See Henri Nouwen, *Reaching Out* (New York: Doubleday, 1975), 57.

4. See Wink, *Engaging the Powers,* 189.

5. Peter Storey, *Our Methodist Roots* (Cape Town: Methodist Publishing House, 1980), 13.

6. Part of the Methodist Rule of Life.

7. Rian Malan, "Confessions of a White South African," *Style* (May 1994), 26.

Trevor Hudson is a pastor of the Northfield Methodist Church, Northmead, South Africa, and a speaker at pastors' conferences in that country. He and his wife, Debbie, have two children, Joni and Mark.